Other works on

THE AWARENESS OF REALITY

By

William Samuel

A Guide To Awareness and Tranquillity

Two Plus Two Equals Reality

The Melody of the Woodcutter and the King

The Child Within Us Lives!

Child Within Journal Notes

We invite the earnest reader's correspondence.

For more information write:

William Samuel & Friends
307 N. Montgomery St.
Ojai, CA 93023
Email: sandy@ojai.net
www.williamsamuel.com

THE AWARENESS OF SELF-DISCOVERY

THE AWARENESS
OF
SELF-DISCOVERY

How To *Live* The Real Identity
By William Samuel

Butterfly Publishing House
Ojai ♥ California

THE AWARENESS OF SELF-DISCOVERY

FIRST EDITION
1970

FOURTH PRINTING
2002

Library of Congress catalog card number: 79-138356

ISBN 1-877999-04-0

Published by

Butterfly Publishing House
William Samuel & Friends
307 N. Montgomery St.
Ojai, CA 93023

Cover Art by Alexandra Bliss Jones

There is no *way* there but to *be* there.

Dedication and Acknowledgments

In the deepest sense, a volume of this nature cannot be dedicated. The reading of it is the Writer writing— so, all these words are your own, your Self-disclosure.

My deep thanks to Mrs. M. D. Reed, faithful collaborator and friend, whose encouragement and editorial assistance has been invaluable in the preparation of this book; and to Mrs. Lynn Dickey who patiently transcribed the mountain of notes made during my woodland wanderings; and to two dear friends, Walter and Emily Cornett whose confidence, encouragement and unstinting love have allowed the meditations of my heart to turn into the *tangible* volume you presently hold in your hand.

Contents

9

CONTENTS

PREFACE

Enlightenment begins with the recognition and acknowledgment of God's absolute *allness.* The basis for this work—its total predicate—lies in the comprehension that Isness (Reality) is single, alone, only and all. Until that acknowledgment is made, no aspect of the Absolute can be understood. Those who come to understand this philosophy are those who make this simple concession for themselves. Oh, but those who are most *helped* by the awareness of God's allness are those who go beyond the intellectual acceptance of the Fact and begin the happy task of *living* it in their daily affairs.

This volume is a companion to A GUIDE TO AWARENESS AND TRANQUILLITY. It will expand the themes presented in that book and permit a degree of insight into the not always easy, but requisite *living* of them.

INTRODUCTION

Gentle reader, nothing about a book of the Absolute can be ordinary. It is not possible to read or write "The Truth" without finding many human values challenged, and this is not at all easy to the old nature of us. The Absolute requires a new view of things. It also requires that the view be made from an entirely new concept of Self— from the standpoint of an identification nothing like the one we have spent a lifetime developing, educating and polishing. Most certainly, the Light of Identity cannot be seen by the human ego, that personal sense of self with which we have grown terribly uncomfortable or else much too comfortable, self-satisfied and unwittingly blinded by. Often it is the discomfort that has us looking for That which the heart tells us must surely exist instead.

The letters included in this volume are taken from my correspondence. They have been altered only enough to prevent disclosing to whom they were sent. There is no intention of disclosing personal confidences, and where it seems I have done so, the necessary permissions have been secured.

The letters used have rendered their service with a "healing" or a comprehension of Light wherein a seed of Truth was effectively "communicated."

Light alone sees 'Light. However, we *are* the Light, consequently we are quite capable of discovering the real Identity—and living it.

Those who correspond with me know my communications often take on the length of essays. They also take on split infinitives, dangling participles, fractured sentences and strange combinations of new words.

To the world, the "communication" of Truth is a unique, mysterious and subtle art—a gift of the Spirit, the Bible says. Inasmuch as the grammar of simplicity, repetition and enthusiasm surely plays a part in the art of communication, I shall not deprive the reader of my enthusiasm nor the opportunity to learn amazing ways to punctuate sentences and misspell words. A good belly laugh is no small "demonstration" in itself for the average super-serious seeker of Truth who sometimes works over-hard searching for the Truth he is already and can't find for looking outside himself.

There is no personal motive for the words in this book! As best I can, I make these statements because it seems proper to do it and less than prudent *not* to do what comes as proper. In truth, there is only one Story of Self-awareness ever being told, here or anywhere. Your own. That story is the here and now You-Experience presently reading these words.

Let me say again: It is the *Awareness of the Absolute,* the Awareness of Self-discovery, that reads these words. We have never been another. This book, therefore, concerns the *identity* you are—God's Self-same awareness which is "you," which is "I," which is the Only. Happy and meaningful reading and happy Self-discovery!

The comprehension of subtle viewpoints appears to require much repetition, the same ideas presented from many angles—softly—vigorously—shockingly—directly and indirectly—sharply, obtusely and sometimes even obversely. Without question, we come to perceive much from our frustrations and the humility of helplessness.

Whatever leads us to the heart-felt comprehension of Light also leads us to the repugnant emptiness of the ego-shell we have all, for good reason, become encrusted by—a shell to be seen for what it is and forsaken. By its contradistinctory nature, it has served to delineate the Real.

The words of this book serve to goad you into the effort of the break out and break away into a New World of Light and Love wherein we find that the old shell with which we were struggling was naught but a *belief.*

Since when does a *belief* have the power and authority to make us hold on to it? It does not. It cannot. And, if you are earnest in your study of this volume, it will not.

CHAPTER I

The Secret Of Communication

This afternoon I held a smooth stone in my hand that existed before a single word had ever been uttered.

Which is more significant: the smooth stone or the words that describe it?

ABOUT WORDS

Dear Mary,

Very often we give too much importance to words. Those who are most devotedly looking for the Truth are frequently the ones most hung up on "This is *relative* or that is *absolute.*" How many times have you heard that? I was the world's worst. As a renegade metaphysician traveling over the universe from sage to Guru to Prince to Practitioner to apostate, no one ever became more entangled in the intellectual concern for words and their precision than I. Pretty soon I found myself with certain expressions I did not dare use in the presence of some people because I was sure my *words* indicated the level of my comprehension. Bosh!

Subtle restrictions of expression—thousands of them—
abound within the *judgmental* framework of *coming-to-
comprehend* the Light rather than *being* the Light.

In our studies here in Mountain Brook, the first thing
we do is to look into the matter of *words,* thence to *come
down* from that ridiculously lofty and arid plateau of
"absolute" versus "relative." *All* words are relative. No
word is absolute. The Absolute that Isness is exists in a
dimension as much beyond words as a melody is more than
a sheet of music or the principle of arithmetic more than
a numeral.

There is an intellectual aspect to Truth, of course,
and words play their part in *that,* but the Real contains
an infinity of subtle essences that is *more* than words,
greater than words. The awakening to *these* is often precluded in our wrestling matches with semantics.

LITTLE BOY LOST

Pondering the enigma of communication one day out
in the back country of my hills, I witnessed the happy reunion of a father and his five-year-old son who had been
lost in the woods for many hours. I knew the boy would
be found—and I knew I knew—but despite the positive
knowing, I was unable to allay the father's fears or bring
him to understand the Truth I saw. Then, even as I wondered—even as I asked about this inability to communicate when it seemed so important to do it—I saw the
little boy and the father find each other.

Oh, such a reunion! A barefoot ragamuffin came run-
ning out of the woods shouting with all his might,
"Daddy! Daddy!" and I saw the father, unashamedly sob-
bing, sweep the child into his arms. All he could say was,
"Hallelujah! Praise God!" again and again. "Hallelujah!
Praise God!"

Then and there, it was my joy to see that *communication* was ever so much more than fancy words, proper grammar and intellectual nuances; more than education and cultured sophistication. I saw uninhibited enthusiasm say more in an instant than all the words of the Encyclopedia heaped upon all the words of the Bible. I saw uninhibited being, stripped of its would-be possessor. In the twinkling of a "Praise God" and a "Daddy, Daddy," I learned that words are just words. Too many are a clutter, and pompous ones a waste. Simple, unpretentious, tender childlikeness—*honesty*—stirs the Heart and overthrows the intellect, leaving the child-we-are in the Father's arms.

Since those days, I have been a child again wandering along the back roads and river banks, enjoying, enjoying. . . Since that time I have known that the intellectual, philosophical presentation of words is not the all-fired important thing I had made of it before. Then and there I determined, as best I could, to end my own use of pompous metaphysical language and attempt to say whatever might be necessary to say in the tender, simple way so *natural* to us all.

This is a portion of the simplicity you and I have discovered, dear reader. It tells the Story to the first and the last alike.

———

"Ah, but what of our dignity if we act so simply?" someone asks.

There has never been more Dignity in all the world than the child who runs to his Father and whispers, "I am home again! I am home again!"

THE CHILD IS UNDERSTOOD

We find a new measure of immediate peace when we end the excessive struggle with words—either our's or the other fellow's. How many times have we listened to the faltering words of children as they poured out their hearts? Didn't we understand all that was necessary to understand? Of course we did! We heard *through* the stutters, the wrong tenses, the misplaced syntax and the mispronounced words. We heard straight through to the simple, honest, tender HEART. It is the Heart that gives utterance to the words we see and hear in the first place, and it is the Heart that understands.

So, as you read these pages, sit easy and look at the paragraphs and chapters in their completeness, in their singleness, in their totality; then, listen to the Heart. It is the Heart that instructs, not the words. The Heart goes beyond words and cannot be fooled. "Behold, I give thee a wise and understanding heart."

———

Laotse, the grand old sage of the East wrote: "The Tao (Absolute) described in words is not the real Tao. Words cannot describe it. Nameless, it is the source of Creation; named, it is the mother of finite images. The Absolute is a vast immeasurable void. Looked for, it cannot be seen; listened for, it cannot be heard; reached for, it cannot be touched... Tao is absolute and nameless— an endless circle ever returning. Serenity is its goal.

"The truly wise man accepts the dualisms of nature and works diligently without allegiance to words... Music and good food will stop the passing stranger, but the Absolute given by way of words seems tasteless and unappealing..."

Then the venerated sage makes what surely must be the understatement of the millenium: "Straight words can seem very crooked."

Some years ago I was honored to be the first American student of a renowned teacher in India. For fourteen days a group of us sat at the feet of this "Master," during which time he spoke not one word—not so much as a grunt—until the final day when he bade us farewell and assured us we had learned much.

And to my surprise, I had. It took months before the seeds of those silent days began to sprout one by one, revealing that there are indeed many things for which the uptight, recondite babble of books and teachers is more hindrance than a help.

There is no one reading this book to whom the Truth has not been revealed many times and for whom the Truth needs only to be *lived*. Additional enlightenment and its *tangible* experience called "healing" come with the LIVING—that gentle meadow of soft grass just beyond the wailing wall of words.

Who built this wall? The same imposter whose role we play as a selfhood apart from Allness.

THE SIGNIFICANCE OF *RE-READING* PHILOSOPHIC MATERIAL

Material of this sort has not been read once until it has been read several times. One cannot possibly discern the full meanings behind these writings with just two or three readings. Oh, yes, the *technical* details can be comprehended in a single reading—if one is intellectually attuned. The "reason and logic" behind the philosophy may be grasped with one or two readings by those who have spent enough time in the study of such material. The worldly *applications* and the immediate surface meanings may very well be found in a single reading— BUT THE LIGHT THAT IS BEING THE AWARE- NESS OF THE WORDS—the Light IDENTITY is— CANNOT BE REVEALED BY WORDS ALONE.

Gentle reader, vainglorious as it may sound, I tell you that I have found a Joy and Tranquillity of Identity that is as far beyond words and worldly appearances as the thunderous sounds of the Celestial Symphony are beyond the ink marks on a sheet of music. The Light I find Identity to be can no more be articulated by these printed words *alone* than the beating of a kettle drum can tell of the immensity of the ocean to a cricket living in a well. But listen, listen: The Light *can* be found. The Symphony *can* be heard because *we are the Symphony* and *we are the Light*.

In the most human terms, wherever the Light has re- vealed Itself, that Light also brings with it its own *means* of being "communicated" and revealed to "others." When- ever the grand Symphony of Identity has been heard, it comes with a means by which its echo, its harmonic or its diametrically opposed discord can be made audible to those who have ears to hear and want to hear it. (The paradox that *some* lines of metaphysical teaching explain is that the discord points an *obverse* finger at the Sym- phony as surely as the echo points directly.)

I very well *know* what I have been given to "com- municate" to my greater sense of Self as I write this book. The Gift I am writing about is the ineffable PEACE Identity is, which comes from the direct apprehension of Awareness as Light—the One Allness AS this Awareness I am. With this apprehension has come, for me, a knowledge of a precise "way," a means, an exact "method" for telling it which I am trying mightily to *do,* even in the face of near insurmountable obstacles to the contrary. But the miracle—the Wonder of Love— is that this communication is happening! It's happening! My earnest "others" are *finding* the Peace I have found. My View of my faithful Self is finding this Peace that is beyond words. You are telling me so in many wonderful ways.

Now, that much said, it seems important to say the following again from a slightly new direction: (Here is some of the repetition I warned you of.) THE SEED OF THIS STUDY IS NOT IN THE WORDS THEMSELVES, NOR NECESSARILY IN THE SPECIFIC ILLUSTRATIONS. It is as much to be found in the *combinations* of the individually complete vignettes and in the changes of *mood* and *tone* between them. It is to be found coming out of the open-hearted FEELINGS (Love!) that these combinations of selections appear capable of inducing in the ego-absented reader. It seems to come forth from the aura of the childlike Love we are; and especially, especially from between the lines *that have been read enough to allow a knowledgeable reading so relaxed and fluid* that YOUR Heart can be heard OVER the words *SIMULTANEOUSLY* adding ITS overtone, *completing* the chord, making that Holy Sound like Gabriel's that heralds the Light—that announces the love and peace which is your heritage and has been your Identity from the beginning. *There is a Holy Music of unbound feeling involved.*

And this is why re-reading is important. Have you not wondered about the power and universal appeal of music and rhythm? The oft repeated prayers and chants of religion are an ancient "method" wherein the intangible

Melody of the Heart ultimately joins the world's external sound of tangibility. It is another aspect of "the two become one," "the inside made as the outside," of "that which ye hear in your *other* ear, *that* preach ye from the housetops."

Once, in China, I was given a simple verse to read and then to give my interpretation. I was ready to give an answer immediately but was informed that I had twenty-eight days to think about it. "Why so long?" asked I, with the usual impatience of a Westerner.

"Because nothing has been read once until it has been read twelve times," was my answer. "Read and re-read."

I did. Twelve times twelve to make twelve readings—and I heard a Melody I could not have heard otherwise. Since then I have known why it is that certain lines in the Bible (or any other book) that have been read countless times will one day, *upon just one more reading*, suddenly take on a grand new significance.

So, reader, with a very gentle touch, read and re-read. If you are in earnest, and act with the earnestness you are, one day *when you least expect it*, you will hear and feel your Heart within complete these words without.

THE SILENCE OF THE SELF

Whatever leads us to the Silence of the Self also leads us to the Light—*to the Light we already are in fact.*

As a boy living on the Mississippi Coast, I often made long afternoon pilgrimages into the back-country bayou land, a veritable swamp, but a wonder-filled place for a boy. It grew water cypress and huge oaks festooned with flowing moss that I likened to the hair of a lovely dream lady.

A railroad skirted the back edge of the swamp marking the usual limit of my penetration. There I had a special place to watch the evening phenomenon of the flowing moss on the live oaks as its color changed in the setting sun from gray to green to nearly yellow, and then for a short moment, to a deep red along its edges as though it were on fire; thence to a dark gray again and nearly black as the sun dropped below the horizon.

Oh, but there was another wonder to delight a boy on those late afternoon journeys. It began when the New Orleans to Mobile train came thundering out of the sun and roared past my vantage point shaking the ground and splitting the air with its hissing steam, pounding wheels and rushing wind. How I tingled with excitement as that metal monster thundered by. Then, when it had passed and its last sounds had clicked away in the East, there followed a silence so still and so soft, so lonely and holy that I could never bring myself to be the first to break it.

It was a childish game, I suppose, but I would sit in the deep silence of the growing twilight until a gull or a killdeer winging its way would break the silence and tell me to go home while there was light enough to find the way.

Were I a teacher at a great university and it fell my lot to give a lecture on Silence, I would want a long freight train on its way to Mobile to come roaring through the lecture hall. From that point there would be no more need for words.

Virtually the same lesson in Silence was repeated for me in China many years later; and with this second lesson I learned that many of the pages of Truth we read (and write) are freight train pages, intended only to make the sounds that follow stand still and soft like great Mississippi oaks, covered with magic moss glowing in the setting sun.

WE CHOOSE SIMPLICITY

Now listen softly. Wisdom comes out of warm quietness and simplicity, not from the bombast of over-
powering words, intellectual Mumbo Jumbo and hard
talk. Knowledge comes out of simple tenderness and
childlikeness. We let weighted concern go! Frustration
and fear have no authority! They cannot alter the Identity being us. We let go the struggle to define the infinitesimal. We end the battle to outline the relationships
of an endless microcosm—foolish task! We come home
to Awareness. We return to simplicity, to the warm
tenderness and inescapable effortlessness of the Already-
Identity Awareness is, right *here*, right *now* reading these
words!

Reader, this is not to laboriously ponder the mysterious
paradoxes as though Wisdom depended on *that*. *This is
to joy in letting go the thinker, and find ourselves the
THINKING of Isness.*

———————

The verse I was to ponder twenty-eight days?

"The same moon shines on ten thousand rivers."

———————

Given the choice of examining an abstruse philosophical
flower of countless variations of color and texture, or a
simple unnamed weed blooming with a frail blossom
along the pathway, we take the weed every time. Its simplicity tells us everything we need to know. Like a child,
the simple Silence of the Self tells It to us as It is.

CHAPTER II

The Hereness And Nowness Of Reality

I do not know of a better way to begin a discussion of the Truth than to call attention to the *here* and *now* of conscious awareness. Our "work" in the Absolute begins with the hereness and nowness of the conscious *awareness* presently reading these words.

Awareness is self-evidently ALL-inclusive. Our "beginning" has to do with the perfect ALLNESS that ALL, GOD, ISNESS is!

THE SINGLENESS OF HERE AND NOW AWARENESS

This here-and-now is perfect. All we are *actually* concerned with is this here and now. The Christian era began with the words, "The time is fulfilled; the kingdom of heaven is at hand." What is this but the statement that Heaven, Harmony, Perfection are *here* and *now* the Fact?

Consider this "here" and "now" a moment: *When* do we read these words? When do we look across the way and see a familiar face? Or any face? When do we see children scampering with their toys? NOW is the "time" that "seeing" takes place. Seeing is NOW.

When do we *hear* the sounds of children at play? When do we hear the voices of friends, the sounds coming from the television, the rustle of leaves underfoot? NOW. Hearing is ever NOW.

When do we catch the smell of breakfast bacon frying or feel the touch of a hand? NOW is the time of all tangible experience, isn't it? Tangibility is NOW—not yesterday, not tomorrow, not even the next moment, but NOW. (And where is the tangible "demonstration" so many are looking for? In the tangible *now* of *this* experience.)

Now consider: *where* is this conscious experience going on? Where do we do all this seeing and listening and experiencing? Not somewhere else—but HERE. And not another time, but NOW. The tangible aspect of conscious awareness is ever HERE and NOW.

Listen again: the here and now are present *as* this consciousness reading these words. *This* is the here-and-now-consciousness that individual Identity is! And this is the only one we are ever concerned with. This is the one we "put in order." *This* is the eye from which we remove the beam.

Actually we have never been concerned with *another* conscious awareness. Even when we think we have been confronted with "another" experience of son, daughter, husband, wife, friend, partner, associate, leader, national figure, potentate, king, Christ Jesus or the hosts of heaven, hell and the universe, the knowledge of these figures and the consciousness of their actions are always *this* conscious awareness even now examining these words! They are every one included "within" and "as" this here and now consciousness that says, "I am!" Who can deny that consciousness lives forever as itself, here and now the eternal moment and infinite place of all that we call "our own" Identity-Experience?

———

"But, Mr. Samuel, my here-and-now is so limited."

The here is infinitely more than a point in space and the now is so much more than a moment in time, despite education's declaration to the contrary. Illumined consciousness reveals ("illumined consciousness" is simply unbound, uninhibited, childlike awareness freed of personal possessorship) an *expanding* consciousness—an expanding hereness and nowness such that we find the strictures of space-time losing their grip and letting us go. Youth reappears *tangibly!* Love blooms anew.

Consequently, simple honesty demands that we come in from a disproportionate time in the boondocks of the not-here and not-now, from the agonizing world of fear we create for ourselves by the too long sojourns into the past or the future. Notice that even these sojourns are now-experiences because the resurrection and reliving of memories is done in the now. We make plans and calculations in the now. We dream in the now. We have missed many tangible wonders in our here and now while wrestling with intangible dreams of a not-now or worrying about events that are not here.

THE BEGINNING

Enlightened philosophy often speaks of finding the beginning and staying there. The beginning for us is this present here and now *awareness.* "Take no thought for the morrow," said the one called Jesus. Sufficient unto this day, this NOW . . . let us get the beam out of THIS eye, this here and now awareness I am, then shall we see clearly . . . Perfection is even NOW spread over the face of the land . . . Beloved, NOW are we the Awareness of Mind. Coming home to the here and now "it doth not *yet* appear what we *shall* be," but we "see" unfolding consciousness AS IT IS (because we *are* unfolding consciousness) and not as it appears in the dream of a not-here, not-now.

Our activity begins with a "coming home" from the far country of not-here and not-now. We "return" to the fact of this here and now awareness ITSELF that presently includes these words. We end the tortuous meanderings of the prodigal and leave the pig sties of his far country. We make a personal discovery of the present consciousness being Identity. This is where we *stay*.

Said Jesus, "Blest is he who shall *stand* at the beginning, and he shall know the end and shall not taste death." Said Laotse, "The Sage is the one who has found the be-ginning and then does not wander from the ways of the ancients." Here is the "secret place." This NOW is the Shekinah. This here and now consciousness is the Holy of Holies into which nothing enters to make a lie.

Oh, but the action of "remaining" here is not the lethargic task one might think. For myself, I became aware quickly and painfully of the old nature's reluctance to give up the ghost. I was sorely shocked at the tenacity of old habit and the lingering smell of smoke. I had to bring myself back time and again to that place where, in actuality, Awareness had never left. I had to bring atten-tion back repeatedly to the conscious recognition of a perfect awareness, the real and only fact of now.

THE NOW IS NEW

Happy new Now, reader. This year, this day, this moment is *new*. The life that reads these words is God's consciousness of being—an eternal Identity about the business of Self-discovery, Self-contemplation and con-sideration, Self-communion and enjoyment. Awareness is

Mind's Self-functioning, not the *personal* activity of one called Bill, Jack, Mary or Jane.

Suppose we resolve to "begin" this New Now looking "with the eyes of God" at the majesty and wonder Isness-as-us is. Let us further resolve to let go, as persistently as we can, Bill's, Jack's, Mary's or Jane's view of things. To do so is to find ourselves letting go the "old man's" fears, frustrations and confusions. To do so is to find ourselves looking at a tangible harmony on the here-and-now-scene —a harmony we can see even when others *won't*. To do so is to live a deep and abiding JOY that cannot be taken from us even if our personal opinions and their pleasures appear to be.

———

The musician begins with the principle of music, not the discord. The mathematician begins with the principle of his science, not the error. WE BEGIN AS THE IMMACULATE, PRISTINE, PURE AND PERFECT IDENTITY WE ARE ALREADY, not the personal sense of things, not the world's ideas, opinions and judgments of things. We "begin" with God, the ALL that Isness is, and rejoice at the wonders this ever new view reveals. We LET that Mind *be us* which IS the awareness of the Christ Truth we are.

———

Reader, I write these words so that during the coming pages we may study together from a common ground—the absolute totality and aloneness of this single, simple and perfect Awareness-we-are. You shall find that an honest, selfless examination of Awareness discloses perfection *already* at hand, merely awaiting our acknowledgment and honest action in accordance.

For additional study on this subject see *A GUIDE
TO AWARENESS AND TRANQUILLITY*: Pages
9 - 26; Page 36, the selection *Happiness is Here;* Page
38, the selection *About Books.*

A LETTER ABOUT AGE AND NOWNESS

My dear friend,

After nearly three weeks away from my green hills, I
return and find your letter waiting for me. How nice to
have homecomings like this!

It is good to hear that you are snapping back. Why
not? You have never been away! We do not have to be
concerned about the events of last night's dream. We snap
home to the *Now* to find that everything is all right.
We live *in* the Now, *as* the Now of perception. We look
around enabled to say, "Behold, everything is very good!"

Awareness does not "retire" but goes on being all
there is to "activity" itself—forever and ever!

Give my back-road and river-bank regards to everyone
you love.

―――――――

It is always NOW—and right now, everything is all
right.

CHAPTER III

Of Principle And Law

There is an all-pervading Principle that rules, regulates and provides for the entire tangible universe. The various laws of physics, mathematics, music, chemistry, etc. are the means of our intellectual (tangible) discernment of this Principle. These laws are so interwoven and bound to one another as to present unassailable proof of the existence of an omnipresent, single Principle being ALL.

The "That" which is *being* this single Principle is "God," the Absolute, the Ineffable, the That beyond a name and greater than the individual laws.

What is the one common denominator for all the known "laws"? It is AWARENESS, the means by which every law is known. The laws, and all that could ever possibly be *known* about them, are included *within* awareness. Awareness is "greater than" laws. Awareness is an aspect of the Ineffable That which is beyond all names and labels, the That Which Is, called Mind or God.

THE ALL-INCLUSIVENESS OF AWARENESS

Every sight we have ever seen has been seen within and as AWARENESS, Mind's action of Self-perception.

Every sound we have ever heard has been heard within and as AWARENESS, the very consciousness that presently reads these words. Every "feeling" that has ever been felt has been another aspect of AWARENESS, Mind's Self-awareness in action.

"Identity" is *awareness.* Identity is not the ego who thinks life (awareness) is his personal possession and/or the gift of God. To believe we are the *custodian* of awareness has us identifying as a potty piece of poppycock "of few days and full of trouble." Furthermore, it has us worshipping a *bestowing* god that doesn't even exist. Mind, you see, doesn't bestow its Self-awareness on "another." Mind IS its OWN awareness. Mind and its action are not two, but one.

———

Nor is Awareness separate from the images within it, any more than the television screen is separate from the cowboys and commercials there.

Therefore, we can see that our identification as awareness ITSELF is not a *withdrawal* from the world, from people or from the adventure of living. It is a withdrawal from our own valued opinions, notions and prejudices of them. To the contrary, this work appears as a revitalized *interest* in everything that appears as conscious identity (Awareness)—and that is everything! As we *live* childlike-awareness-being-effortlessly-aware, we find our daily experience *expanding* into undreamed of new action —*plus the strength and means necessary for that action.*

———

Sitting on a riverbank down in Alabama one day, I lived my newly discovered identity as Awareness and whispered of it to myself. I whispered so softly the reeds beside my feet could scarcely hear—yet that whisper was heard "clean to the other bank."

Reader, live identity like a whisper. You will be heard around your world. Even around the Universe.

"Comprehendest thou this?"

THE INCLUSIVENESS OF AWARENESS INCLUDES "OTHERS"

Once a lecturer told me of the awful fear he felt every time he stood before a large audience. "Eventually most public speakers get over this sort of thing," he said, "but I'm getting worse. If I do not get to the root of this problem soon, I will have to stop lecturing."

Awareness *is* all that awareness includes. Talking to myself, I suggested that "he" look out and see his audience as the mirrored image of himself. He certainly had no need to stand there and quake in the harmless presence of *himself.*

This was not just a gimmick to get over the fear of people, I told him, because the day we honestly perceive those who listen to us as aspects of the Self-I-am, we find them listening, understanding, comprehending and discovering what we are talking about. It is senseless human dishonesty and trepidation to expect anything less!

Well, he saw the point intellectually. But more important, he perceived that a "healing" in the *tangible* scene at hand required that the newly perceived point be put to the test and *lived,* actually, tangibly, right *where* the problem appeared to be producing its fear.

So he had a little card printed that he placed on the lectern. It said: "THIS EVENING I AM GIVING THIS LECTURE TO MYSELF FOR MY OWN SELF-DE-LIGHT. SINCE I KNOW MY SUBJECT VERY WELL

AND ENJOY IT VERY MUCH, I WILL DAMNED
WELL UNDERSTAND AND APPRECIATE WHAT I
HAVE TO SAY. FURTHERMORE, I MAY EVEN BE
OVERWHELMED AND APPLAUD MYSELF VIGOR-
OUSLY."

Since that day he has been around the world talking to
an ever proliferating and appreciative self-image.

We can all make the same trip.

Dear John,

I am just back from Maryland where I gave a series of
talks to a happy group at a lovely farm called Dayspring—
green fields of grass surrounded by hardwood forests of
hickory and towering white oak the likes of which are
seldom seen anymore. For three days we talked at the
lodge and walked the fields together—barefoot even!
We sat on the grass, on the porch, under the trees, just
Awareness being aware. There was a pond with a log
across it and wild flowers blooming along the pathway
leading there . . .

It was a grand experience of Love and Light—of awaken-
ings—healings—discoveries. And why not? As simple,
credulous Awareness, I was the Seeing of the Light I am.
All the laughter was mine. The tears of Joy were mine.
I was talking to myself and understanding.

THE "HEALING VIEW" BEGINS WITH ALLNESS

We begin every consideration from the standpoint of
the ineffable, perfect ISNESS which is the first, last, single
and only FACT of Being. We begin with THAT
WHICH IS. We begin with REALITY. We begin with
"God." We do *not* begin with the problem even though

it is usually an apparent difficulty, a discontent or something adjudged incorrect (or not good enough) that has us scurrying after a knowledge of ISNESS.

But from whence cometh the scurrier? Granting the *onlyness* of the single and only primordial FACT, just who is this "we" who senses an apparent difficulty? Who is this one who makes the effort to begin every consideration from the standpoint of Isness? Really, just who is the one who asks the question from the position of one who doesn't know the answer? Where have we gotten the notion we are such an identity as that? If we do not believe in a selfhood apart from Perfection, why are we playing the role, pretending to be one in darkness looking for the Light?

Those who are in earnest about this study must answer these questions and answer them to their own satisfaction. Get out your private notebook. Begin from the standpoint of an already perfect Allness (just as you begin every mathematical consideration from the automatic position of a perfect principle of mathematics being the "answer" to every question concerning that principle). Then, determine for yourself just where an ignorant, struggling identification fits into the picture of an *omniscient* and *only* Reality.

I have found that starting with the error only perpetuates the belief of the error. I have found that starting with the claim, the agony, the fear, frustration, grief or threat of grief only has the one who would operate from such a position *stuck* with that position until the intellectual futility of it literally whips the misconception of Identity from the temple.

"I" look away from the error long enough to reestablish *conscious* identification in and as the only actual (and possible) identity on the scene—Reality's Self-awareness *itself*—and then, THEN, *I am able to look on the*

"error" *to see what it really is.* I can assure you it is
never, never what it appears to be to the misidentity, that
ego-intellect who believes itself an entity apart from the
One.

Try it and see for yourself.

CONCERNING CHILDREN

Someone writes wondering about the appearance of
ill children in the world. "Why should these innocents
suffer so?" he asks.

Reader, ponder the following points gently. Listen
to the heart without allowing the intellect to enter in.
(The declarations of the Absolute are seldom in accord
with the opinions of the world. Neither do they coincide
with the usual dictates of "common sense." On the other
hand, there is no limit, *there is no limit at all,* to the
Heart's ability to perceive the Absolute and understand it.)

Isness is all; perfectly and exclusively so.

All is *all.*

There is no imperfect child in all existence.

There is one child only—that one being THIS Identity
we are (I am) who presently reads these words.

THIS simple, credulous Child-Identity-is is infinitely
perfect and perfectly *infinite.*

(Do those "innocents" appear *outside* this Awareness-
Identity-is, or within us? They most certainly are not
separate nor apart from the consciousness that perceives
them.)

How is INFINITY seen?

Via SELF-delineation, including specific, tangible form.

"People" are the infinite identification of *Awareness,*
appearing in Self-delineated form.

"As *I* be lifted up . . ." *here,* perceiving the real and unbound Child *I* am, then my self-delineated form of Awareness "out there" ". . . is lifted up likewise and drawn unto me."

This Identity we are is AWARENESS, the *action* of Mind, God.

Its "purpose" (*Our* reason for being!) is to delineate itself, Deity's SELF-Awareness in action. And this is our heritage! This is our inescapable Identity, *already* the only fact of Allness. All is already infinite. Infinity is already all.

HOW DO WE VIEW PEOPLE?

"I" view "people," regardless of their appearing, as GOD'S AWARENESS GOING ABOUT GOD'S BUSINESS OF BEING AWARE OF THE INFINITE QUALITIES, CHARACTERISTICS AND ATTRIBUTES OF GOD.

Can my "others" be *less* than this?

Can "people," the infinite delineation of Awareness, be less than perfectly Self-conscious?

This is the view that allows "me" to see wonder and beauty where "others" still see things they speak of in terms of horror, frustration or dismay. This view sees the Child-I-am, either "here" or "there," as *not guilty*— as *not bound* by the judgments of the world—as FREE, and freely about the Father's business of Self-awareness. This view does not condemn Self for a human determination of imperfection—and, as appearances go, this view frees and "heals" the Child-I-am "out there."

The healing purview of the Absolute is not limited to the "healers" of the world, to the "practitioners" or metaphysicians. *This is your heritage as well.* You are yourSELF the perfect functioning of everyone you see—even as the one in the center of the house of mirrors is the substance and form of his countless images appearing as delineations of a single selfhood. To perceive the self-perfection of the single one at the center is to joy in the harmony, the beauty and the love of Perfection's "out there" as well as "here." Be the faithful witness! Take up your sceptre and reign!

The view of the image is ever here as I.

". . . and as I be lifted up . . ." said the enlightened prophet from Galilee.

———————

Dear Mary,

Ruby and I frequently take a group of so-called "retarded" children for an outing aboard Lollygog. I assure you there is nothing retarded there! We look on "others" as awareness simply being very much aware—and I can tell you these children see everything, hear everything, feel and enjoy everything! We are not about the business of determining *how* images are supposed to look, walk or talk. Rather, we are in the business of seeing images-out-there as *what* they are: perfect images, doing what they are supposed to be doing—and that perfectly! How we love those beautiful children and how they enjoy the days with us. Oh, dear Mary, how blest you are to be able to work with your young people every day!

CHAPTER IV

Imagination, Reality And Judglessness

When an oppressive situation is at hand and tranquillity appears to be threatened, there are many things we can do that will "heal" the situation—and quickly. For instance, we can open the doors of imagination to the real and beautiful.

This requires an act of strength because our every intellectual tendency is to NOT leave the scene of misery but to hang in there and do battle with it. Anything less is called intellectual cowardice and labeled "escapism" by the world. But we let go the apparent scene long enough to let imagination carry us back to the Principle wherein no inharmony exists. Soon we touch an area of gentle relief within ourself and we can be certain we will shortly be lifted up, out of gloom, into the atmosphere of the Absolute.

This journey of Awareness is helped considerably if we write it into words as we go along. The act of writing carries us more deeply into the Within where tranquillity is.

Here is an example of such a journey:

THE LIVE OAKS AND THE MOUNTAIN COVE

Once I lived beneath the massive oaks of the Mississippi coast. Those oaks are there yet. Even this instant when an oppressive situation is attempting to make me yield to it, I know those giant trees are there, mighty monarchs, massive and green, festooned with flowing moss. Yellow flickers, wax wings and cardinals dart among them. Gray squirrels scamper along their high branches jumping with measured grace from limb to limb. This very instant that scene is one of peace and tranquillity. The air is moist and sweet there. A gentle peace holds the scene in silence.

Now I see a winding road that skirts a mountain cove. Hickory, sycamore and pine line the field below. Crisp mountain air bathes the scene and bees hum past in swift arcs carrying the day's pollen to the hive and home. A deer peers cautiously from the woodland and drinks from a cool stream at his feet. The scene is just a scene being a scene—tangibly "there" in that mountain glade; intangibly "here" as a sparkling, pristine vision in the Mind's Eye that Awareness is. "Here," I see, is merely the "place" the outside becomes the inside, the inside, outside.

Awareness is the Mind's eye, the Mind's ear. It is the whole (holy) gamut of perception. Awareness is Mind's function functioning—for which *Mind* is responsible.

Ah, but here is the point I have been so slow to perceive, so reluctant to admit. MIND is responsible, not the ego-me. For how many years have I played at being God, *custodian* of Awareness, *manipulator* of the sights and sounds that comprise this Identity-I-am? What wonders are mine each time I make the sacrifice and come out from the custodian's role to let Mind be this functioning I am.

What does this have to do with the mountain cove or the trees along the Southern shore? It has to do with the *consciousness* of the trees and fields, the oceans, the Pleiades and the stars in far places. It has to do with this Identity-I-am, *God's Self-cognizance.*

OUR TENDENCY TOWARD DUALISM

We are wont to have a vague Spiritual universe to dream and talk about—a universe wherein no imperfection exists and one to which we may appeal to rectify the malappearances in our tangible world. We are eager to have a visionary heaven, yet the place where we expect to *see* Harmony's evidence is ever in the here and now of tangibility. All this while we are *looking* at Harmony's very trees, stones and desert places, calling them dreams, calling them unreal, trying to heal them. We would have a dualism despite ourselves—a real and an unreal, a heaven and an earth, a truth and an error, an above and a below.

"He who has ears to hear, let him hear," said Jesus. "When you make the two one. When you make the above as the below, the first as the last, the inside as the outside . . ."

We do not discard the scene at hand in some grand metaphysical sweep, calling it all unreal. We turn from it—but we turn only long enough to see it is not the *scene* that lies, but the *judge* of it, the liar we play when we separate ourselves from Awareness (the Identity we are) to play at being God, the director of Awareness. Images within the scene have neither the value nor the authority the liar gives them. *I look out and see that Heaven is this very Scene at hand!*

The agony that began the exercise of imagination turns out to be something else. Tranquillity lets me see *what—* and act accordingly.

Dear John,

As you very well know, only Truth comprehends Truth, and this very Awareness I Am (you are) is the *comprehending* in unceasing action! Awareness has *no* responsibility (no guilt) for *what* is "seen" (or *not* seen) nor the "condition" of it! Awareness is simply *aware.* It does not *judge* the "thing" included "within" Itself. Awareness beholds the blossom or the little girl, the mountain brook or the evening star, without judgment, concern, criticism or comparison. Awareness *Itself* is simply being aware; busy being the *Infinite Intelligence* that knows Itself to be beholding Itself.

———

"Judge not," says the Christ. "I judge no man . . . *Cease Ye* from judgment . . . think *not* . . . in that moment when ye think (judge) not . . ." These admonitions are fulfilled only by *ceasing* to identify as a judge of good and evil, thereby *ceasing to make value judgments.* We stop acting as if duality were an actual fact of Being.

God, Isness, does not *really* relinquish this activity (Awareness) to another identity who judges all that is perceived.

———

Mine has been a wonderful "experience" since I stopped playing the part of a judge! This is not as hard to do as the world says it is. The effort comes from thinking, planning, calculating, comparing and attaching values to everything. "I will give thee *rest,*" says the Christ. "My yoke is *easy* . . . *Cease* ye from judgment . . . take no thought . . . consider the lilies of the field; they toil not, neither do they spin . . . behold, the Kingdom of Heaven is *at hand . . . here . . . now!*" This is so! This is a fact!

———

Truth has to do with our very Identity. Should something seem to be untrue (in a book, lecture or anywhere
else) it has nothing to do with us, nothing to do with
Truth. When it is so regarded, it ceases "seeming." All
"seeming" has to do with something that does not fulfill
a judge's expectations.

Within the totality and onlyness of *God is All,* where is
there room for another who judges everything? Though
we may play the role of a judge, and in the eyes of that
role suffer the consequences, our actual identity is not
that one! We are not *really* the one who says this is good
and that is bad, I want this and don't want that.

"Who made me a judge?" asks the Christ.

Most often it seems we must discover the agony we
bring upon ourselves through misidentification before
we are willing to forsake the ways of that misidentification.

The "Last Judgment" the Bible speaks of is not the
stuff and nonsense theology has made of it, but it is
something. Within yourself you will know the "last judgment" when you cease to make judgments. It is literally
your own *last condemnation* of the things you see and
hear—of the "feelings" you feel!

Do you think it is *impossible* to end your personal value
judgments? I assure you it is not. We begin by *refusing*
to dislike a thing—refusing to *feel* that an object of perception has more or less value than any other. Soon we find
ourselves laughing at life-long irritations and viewing the
world in a new light.

"Who made me a judge?" asked Jesus. "I judge *no*
man," he said. He admonished us to "go and *judge no
more,* lest you be judged by the same judgment!"

So you see, *Now* is the time to move from the arena of philosophic speculation (talk) and have our "doing" correspond with our knowing. It is more effortless than you might imagine. It isn't long until we realize that the effort behind life's continuing struggle comes from excessive thinking, planning, calculating—judgment making!

CHAPTER V

The Difference Between Distinction And Judgment

All of us who have lived this philosophy have found that we are able to see the immediate end of much personal agony the instant we pull the rug from under our former value judgments. It is our continual "This is good and that is bad; I love this and hate that; this is valuable and that worthless; this, dangerous, that, safe, etc." that precludes either a clear perception or a full enjoyment of the *perfect* NOW.

It has very often been our determination that something is "good" that would have us cherishing it, lusting after it, struggling to own it, guard it, worship it or bemoan its loss. It is equally our value-judgment that something is bad that has had us hating it, running from it, struggling to get rid of it or crusading against it. The very same "thing" is frequently loved by one and hated by another, so clearly, the agony is not in the "thing" but in the judgment of it. By and large, value judgments bestow either positive or negative value to the "thing," be it a sight, sound, person, place, event, feeling or idea, and it is a value we do not need to make nor give to the image.

We have found our ability to subdue value-judgments easier said than done. It is an ingrained habit of long standing—*but it is possible to break it,* nonetheless, and the "results" are *immediate* from the moment we *begin to try.*

The primary "way" to see images as *neither* good nor bad is to perceive the absolute Fact that they are included within awareness AS awareness, and that they are all, equally, the same "substance"—Awareness, Spirit, Mind, Isness. The "value" lies with Awareness, not the image it includes. To give the image a value that belongs *here* as this very Identity awareness is, is to give away the dominion that is rightfully ours and thereby yield ourselves servants to obey the image. The "value" ever resides *here* as the ineffable That which is being this Consciousness I Am.

Since the publication of A GUIDE TO AWARENESS AND TRANQUILLITY, I have had countless communications telling me of the new freedom that has consciously presented itself as the consequence of this simple act of being less judgmental and critical of everything. Our past study of metaphysics, having had little to say about the silly and wasting tactic of value-judgment, led many of us into that hypercritical arena of dichotomy and polarization: "This is real and that is only a dream going on; this is Truth and that is error; this is absolute and that is dualistic, etc." The tangible "consequence" of such a course of action leaves us with no alternative but to look about and see that polarization developing as our mirrored world of tangibles.

Whether we were conscious of it or not, the continuing judgment of everything has constituted an awful effort. The end of the habit comes as a grand relief.

THE INCREASE OF SENSITIVITY

I would like to make clear a wondrous fact concerning this matter of judglessness. Many have found it already and have written in great excitement to tell me of it, but it seems to be a point difficult to understand by those who have only given the action of living judglessly a half-hearted try. Many a puzzlement can be cleared up when we understand this: To the extent that we stop placing good-bad values on our images of awareness, OUR ABILITY TO DISTINGUISH INCREASES, and increases enormously.

There is a great difference between value-judgments and distinctions—a difference not easily understood until we actually get underway and begin *ending* our judgments. *Then* the great difference becomes apparent and, as it does, our actions follow suit, often to the wonder (and criticism) of the world.

To make this point crystal clear, let it be said again: The ability to *distinguish* increases as *judgment ends.* Distinguish what? New *sights* we have been unconscious of before; new *sounds* we have never consciously heard before; *feelings* we long since thought had vanished with the years. But more, we find an ever growing ability to distinguish new things in areas not recognized as containing new things—somewhat as if we had long been familiar with a bowl of glass marbles, heretofore seen simply as "marbles" but now, bit by bit, seen to be marbles of different *sizes, colors and designs*—all these apparent *distinctions* that others seem not to see at all! Yes, perception "becomes" clear and acute. An intuitive alertness of a new kind develops. Inevitably, the wonder is how we could have been so stupid as to miss these things before.

But, lo, with this positive phenomenon in one direction, comes another in the opposite. (Contradistinctions! The "means" by which Singleness is tangibly known). This new ability to perceive distinctions (arriving as the natural consequence of subduing judgmental living) *is often viewed as a judgmental action by "others"!* — in particular, by those of us who have intellectually arrived at the advantages of judglessness but have not given it a real try. "The less judgmental or critical I am," someone writes, "the more I am accused of it! Why?" Another question comes: "Why should I expect mental clarity and feelings of youth to increase as I stop living judgmentally? If I could believe that, I would give it a try."

When the intellect understands a point, it is occasionally willing to concede it. The following illustration has proven helpful to "make clear upon the tables" the why and how of the tangible "results" that come from hanging the apple back on the tree. At the same time it will point out the differences between judgment and distinction— and why our new found ability to distinguish *appears* as judgment to "others."

Reader, put yourself INTO this illustration. Take your present lingering likes, dislikes, wants and wishes into this analogy and see how and why they are, everyone, monumentally *more* than you suspect.

THE ILLUSTRATION OF THE DARK FRINGE AT THE EDGE OF THE FIELD

Suppose we have been raised since youth to be frighten- ed of the forest on the other side of the field. Because we *believed* what we were told of the forest (by parents or school, church or society) we have never gone near it and, in the distance, that forest appears to be a dark fore- boding fringe at the edge of the field. We have judged the forest to be bad. We are afraid of it and stay away. Keep this picture in mind as we proceed.

See how fear limits our action. We do not go in *that* direction.

Is family or society to blame for our fear? Are they guilty? They may tell us incorrectly that the forest is bad but it is we who accept what "they say" as true. Our acceptance of the value-judgment is *our* doing and it is our own belief in the lie that has us suffering.

Our first consideration should be what WE-AS-IDEN-TITY-*HERE* accept as Fact; what Identity-HERE believes, and not what should or should not come forth from the sundry sand-foundationed teachers out there. We cannot know what to do constructively about the authorities and governments of the world until we have gotten things straight as Identity HERE first.

Note, especially: our living the belief (and "suffering" from it) has surely served as the means to *KNOW beyond intellectuality* that Authority exists HERE AS I, not there as that. (Are we going to forever condemn the events that have served us so well?)

———

Now we take the illustration another step. Some aspect of our ever new and "expanding" Self comes along and tells us that the dark fringe at the edge of the field is neither good nor bad but that an unnecessary value-judgment makes it seem so. Something within us responds and whispers, "It is so! It is only a forest being a forest!" What happens now?

Whenever the Heart blooms in Light, there is a lessening of illusory fear. The dark fringe seems less ominous and we are not *quite* so afraid to walk in that direction. Former restrictions are vanishing but (notice) *old patterns of action remain.* The *habit* of *not going* near the forest remains until we put our new Light and freedom into action. Reader, for me, facing former judgments has been a matter of girding up the loins, flouting former ways and walking across the entire field, row by row, to remind myself anew and again that the Power is not *there* with *that*, but *here* as *Identity*, thence finally to *know beyond doubt* that the fear was actually without foundation.

———————

Listen: Herein lie the reasons *why* judgless living so wondrously sharpens and quickens us, increasing our sensibilities beyond all we have ever known: What happens to the dark fringe as we live judglessly, walk across the field and insist on our freedom? (That is, what happens when we *face up to* our old fears without our former beliefs of them?) The forest becomes more distinct. It changes color. Soon we are aware of many things we did not see before—individual trees, shrubs, flowers. We hear sounds of nature we did not know existed. And in time we see that some trees are tall and some short, some old and some young. Some bend like the willow; others are unyielding like the oak. What was once a single, unqualified "bad" is seen to be a *transcendent* infinity.

These are not *judgments* hoving into view, reader. These are distinctions that our fearless living of judglessness has allowed us to become aware of. There is a vast difference between distinctions and judgments—distinctions being qualities and attributes (of Isness) precluded from conscious (tangible) view by judgment and apparent only when that judgment ends *and the former fear faced*. Distinctions are the reasons that lie behind the appearances.

What was once a miserable dark fringe is now seen to be a forest composed of oak, hickory, pine and sassafras, each different, each beautiful, each doing its part to make a perfect forest a perfect forest. We see varieties of things we never knew existed. Our ability to distinguish has increased enormously. *The absence of fear* (or desire) has allowed us to experience what seems to the old point of view to be an *expanding* of awareness, an *increasing* sensibility, a proliferating capability to distinguish—see, hear, feel—things as they are, rather than as they seem. And they inevitably transcend anything the fearful view could have dreamed.

What once seemed to be the fearful forest of a retarded child is perhaps seen to be a faithful teacher at whose feet we sit in awe and wonder, WE the student, the child a very faithful and wonderful teacher! What once seemed to be a dark forest of family friction or marital inharmony is seen to be a new aspect of Light and Love coming to be acknowledged. What once seemed to be the woodland of penury, poverty, woe and want is recognized as the perfect condition which brought us to the very enlightenment going on right HERE, right NOW. The *reasons* for the dark fringe begin to appear. Enigmas that had been painful before begin to vanish quietly, imperceptibly, as the morning mist along the river vanishes before the sunshine and gentle wind out of the West. We hold hands and sing. We hear angels laughing.

DUALISM AGAIN

Suppose "two" of us have been looking at the dark fringe at the edge of the field and each has heard of the advantages of ending incessant criticism and value-judgment, but only one girds up the loins to walk across the field. What happens? The brave one tells of his ever increasing ability to distinguish oak from elm only to find that his distinctions appear as judgments to the one still on the sideline who cannot see them. He is likely to hear himself asked why he doesn't practice what he preaches about judglessness—and this is the abuse nearly always suffered by those who *dare* put their Light into action. There are many, for one reason or another, who are determined to defend their particular theory of the forest—even as we did before our theory gave way to Fact. But, "Blessed are ye when men shall revile you and persecute you and say all manner of evil against you falsely. . ." What comes as criticism of our action can in no way gainsay the JOY of freedom we FEEL and KNOW about beyond guess-work. Unless we choose to let it!

In the end, we have no alternative but to stop worrying about what "they say" and concern ourselves with naught but this HERE and NOW Identity, our own SELF-experience and the integrity thereof. When we are seen entering and leaving the forest, we will surely be asked about our views by those who are sincerely interested— the only ones who listen anyway. Most often, the old nature of us only wants its cherished opinions verified and strengthened. It is very fast to lower the boom on anything that doesn't.

But even this is just part of the fun of walking across the field. As we actually begin to subdue the old habit of making judgments and as we recede from the old views of our former beliefs (the world's view), we see those old beliefs in a new light too. Finally, at the edge of the once feared forest, we TURN AROUND and see the whole human scene in ITS singleness, amazed to discover that even *that* is transcendentally more than we ever dreamed it could, couldn't, should or shouldn't be.

Reader, the way "across the field" is to see Identity as all there is to both field and forest. It is to see that there is not a *real* judgmental "me" who continues in the need to be fearful of some aspect of himself in order to "learn" thereby. We see ourselves as Infinite Wisdom who *knows,* not an ignorant tub of trembling jelly who needs to *learn.*

There is no way there but to *be* there. *There is no way there but to be there!*

But we do not use this knowledge as an excuse to continue condemning the forest nor rail at others who appear to.

LETTERS ABOUT JUDGLESSNESS

Thank you for your letter, dear Mary...
...and for the word that you are finding "my" book helpful. Whatever you find therein that strikes a responsive chord has to do with your own identity. The credit does not lie with me or the book, but with the consciousness that "reads" it. It has to do with You.

About judgments—and listen softly: It is the old nature of us, "the old man," the misidentification, etc., viewing itself as an entity "separate and apart" from *allness* who finds it important to battle its way through the thicket. The fact is clearly apparent that *God* does not have to do that—and God's action, God's activity, just happens to be the very Awareness (consciousness) presently reading these words. This is IT! The honest, effortless Identity-being-I (us) is awareness *itself*—for which *God* is "responsible," not a personal sense of self, not an ego, not a struggling prodigal who must search the crevasses for sustenance.

Oh, yes, we still make all manner of distinctions and business determinations. The "judgments" that are "the

damning weight of Job" are those we make as a personality—those that say, "This is good; that is bad—therefore,
this is to be desired; that is to be hated, healed, gotten
rid of, changed, etc."

We continue to make distinctions and differentia-
tions: "This appears to be a happy customer; that, an
area requiring attention, etc." but we bring the curtain
down on attaching more *value* to any one appearance
than another. It is our attachment of "value out there"
that has us writhing in agony over what an "out there"
appears to do or not do.

In this way, not so caught up in the struggle with fear
and foreboding, we are able to look on our business
affairs with greater perspicacity than before and see
what to do.

I have spent a lot of time with this letter because—
looking on your letter without judgment, without personal
evaluation and without feeling that Allness is anything
less than perfect—it seems to be right, fitting, proper,
correct (or whatever word one wishes to use to connote
tending to one's business as it comes to him to tend) to
write you this clarification.

"Comprehendest thou this?"

I know you do because infinite intelligence itself—
the only wisdom in all existence—is the Identity you
are.

Dear Friend,

To the business of your coming lawsuit: Have no
concern for the outcome. The verdict, either way or
none at all, *does not have the authority to "upset" you.*

Who sits in agony over the anticipated (or hoped for)
outcome of a television story? Does the television screen

develop internal pressures when the pictures shadowed within it are sad stories of unrequited love, money lost in the market, shoot-outs or lawsuits between disgruntled images?

These are not frivolous questions. Mull them over. Answer them for yourself before the event with the court. You see, the awareness that sees this very letter is Deity's awareness of Deity—it is not possessed, contained nor dictated to by one called Samuel or anyone else. Most especially it is not held in bondage by the images it contains *within* it, be they "people," "sounds" or "feelings."

Does the television screen have anything to do with *what* images are shown forth within it?

Awareness does not "break into consciousness;" Awareness is the *activity* of Consciousness, the Godhead. Deity is already beholding its perfect *unjudged* and *unvalued* attributes. *Who or what can separate consciousness-being-aware from the awareness consciousness is being?*

No matter how much we may want to act the ego-judge who places values on the sights and sounds within awareness, we cannot forever hold onto and act a ghost identity.

Gird up your loins. Dare to challenge the values the old nature has placed on the sights, sounds and feelings of Awareness. That which we have called "bad" is not bad at all and that which has been called "good" is not good. These are but opposite ends of the dualism that springs from the judge's view.

We do not do away with the images we do not like; we do not alter them to fit a prescribed picture ("I hope the judge dismisses the case"). We see them as they are—just sights being sights.

Every form is Isness being form. Isness is the value—not the image-form out there! So we learn to stand before every picture unmoved, our equanimity undisturbed. When we finally muster the courage to do this—when we DO this—*actually do it*—we stop being upset by that which we once gave the authority to lead us around by the nose.

With kindest regards,

Dear Mary,

I know you will find the practice of judglessness to be an amazing undertaking. It leaves us with a warm, child-like, free and unencumbered view that no longer struggles between relative and absolute, good and evil, right or wrong. It leaves us being what we have really been all the while—Deity's awareness of Deity's self-evident allness. And it does not leave us with two views—one spiritual and one human—but just *this* view which is *It!* Yes, it is so, Mary, perception of these words, here and now, is Being's Self-awareness in action. Happy, carefree, eternally *youthful* action! Why, it could not be otherwise!

Dear One,

How beautiful your letter! Isness, God, is the Solitary, the Alone, the All. This Only One is Self-conscious, and that Self-consciousness is Identity. Within all of All there is no other identity. Self-consciousness functioning is Awareness. The conscious awareness reading these words is the functioning of Deific Self-consciousness. THIS is the Identity "I" am. Never, never have I been a posssessor, container, lord and master of Awareness! Never! Even if once I believed myself a possessor of "Awareness *in me*," never was Awareness-I *that* one!

Deity perceiving Itself is "what" Awareness is—and when the ludicrous attempt to play the role of dictator-possessor of Awareness ends, "...we see, even as we are seen."

Now, you may happily "watch" without judgment anymore—without having to call this good and that bad, this real and that unreal, this awake and that sleeping. Now you may watch the "return" of freshness and vigor and youth and sparkle—yes, and SEE the lines of care disappear—not that this is a mark of accomplishment, for it isn't. "All that matters," as one of old wrote, "is the new creation."

Yes, as you have discovered, Tranquillity is your Identity—not something you feel, experience, or put on like an overcoat over an untranquil false-identity. It is inevitable that you should see this, for the simple reason that you *are* this Tranquillity already.

It seems a mistake to allow personality into the picture on *our* part. Why? Because we are often tempted to judge what is said by the look of the one who says it, or the sound of his voice. It is written that no one would ever read Goethe or Shakespeare who had listened to them first. This is as preposterous and stultifying as to judge a book by the typewriter it was written on or the Ten Commandments by the quality of Mount Sinai's stone. There is but *one* real personality; that one is God—God, who is being all there is to this Single and Only Awareness I am (you are).

As judgment ends, the infinity of Identity distinguishes Itself as Us.

CHAPTER VI

Unpossessed Awareness

Once upon a time there lived a working man who detested coffee. His wife did not know this, however. He had never told her. She loved coffee very much and took great delight in packing a Thermos of the stuff in his lunch box every morning.

He always carried the box and Thermos to work, but being a frugal man, brought them home again in the evening, the Thermos of coffee still untouched. Then, to save a penny, and because his wife loved coffee as much as he detested it, he poured the java back into the coffee pot when she wasn't looking. He was excused the evening coffee on the grounds that it kept him from sleeping well.

One night the wife dreamed that her husband was unfaithful to her. The next night she had the same dream. It angered her, but she said nothing. A week or so later the dream happened a third time, causing her much jealousy and anguish.

"It is true," she thought. "It *must* be true. The worm is unfaithful to me!" So, she set out to avenge herself. This she did by putting a pinch of arsenic in his Thermos every morning until she killed herself.

At the husband's trial of acquittal, the judge said, "It is always the same. Those who believe the dream murder themselves."

The primary prop upholding the dream is the *belief* that the awareness (life) reading these words is the personal possession of an ego, a personality, a selfhood separate and apart from Single Isness. The flat-earth belief has been foisted upon us that we are the recipients of life and the religions of the world are busy perpetuating that belief by having us worship a *bestowing*, life-*giving* god that doesn't even exist.

Are these atheistic or "Communistic" statements? They are *not!* Not even remotely. We are not proclaiming the non-existence of "God." We are about the happy business of disclosing that the very life reading these words is the Life that God IS, Reality IS, Isness IS. We are pointing out the Light which reveals that life (Life) *is* "God," closer than fingers and toes, closer than breathing. A single, divine, all-inclusive awareness is who and what we are *already* — and we do not have to go begging and importuning our way up the leg of an imaginary god via the rituals and procedures of a world that is included *within* awareness.

Since when is the Deific Awareness of Being dominated by that which it includes within Itself? By analogy, the tail is wagging the dog, for St. Peter's sake; the images on the screen are pulling the television set around by its tubes; the dream is whipping the dreamer to death. Oh, but for a purpose. His growing nightmare awakens him!

Thank you for your great letter, dear Rebecca...

...it is apparent that yours is a happy home. You have noticed too, that lightness is appreciated wherever love is tangibly apparent. I have always wondered about the staid presentations of Truth—the restraining dignity, the whispered utterances, the voices that never wavered from the sonorous and saccharine when all the while the Love I felt was bounding like a free-spirited colt turned to new pastures. Love breaks forth in tender tones, certainly—and in a serious, dignified manner if that is what appears appropriate at the moment—but the Joy Truth *is* appears unfettered and free to me, unbounded by convention, incapable of becoming the tool of a dignitary. It laughs and teases like a child. Tall though they are, my stately pines dance in a storm. So do your majestic redwoods. And so do you and I and all the unencumbered and unpossessed.

A monumentally helpful point for metaphysicians to "get straight" is the simple, basic and very gentle fact that awareness—consciousness—is *God's* Self-perception in action, not the personal tool of an ego. In our work here, awareness, consciousness and life (Life) are synonymous terms. Awareness is the action of God, the activity of Mind, the Life that God is. Indeed, the consciousness presently reading these words, that perceives the scene outside, that hears the rustle of pots and pans in the kitchen and gathers in the evergreen thoughts and feelings of the Season, is the living that *God* is, the awareness that *Mind* is, the all and only perceiving of *Deity* going on. This consciousness right here and now is the life divine that never ends—the awareness of God.

There are not two awarenesses, one that belongs to Bill, Mary, John or world, and another somewhere afar off, marvelous and mysterious, that belongs to God. All there is to "mortal mind" is the now-to-be-discarded notion that the consciousness reading this page belongs to a finite personality with a responsibility for "his" experience. Consciousness, awareness, "seeing," "perceiving"— or whatever else it may have been called—is *GOD'S* responsibility and God's consciousness in action.

Conscious of what? Of all there is to be conscious of: the infinity of all that God, Reality is. THIS life *we* are is God's own Self-appraisal, God's Self-seeing, Self-knowing, Self-being.

Reader, listen softly: Awareness and life are one. Relax for a moment and *admit* the simple, gentle Fact that All is *all*, hence the consciousness that even now surveys this printed page is the goal of the sages from time immemorial, the LIVING that God is, the Life Divine that neither begins nor ends. See this! Comprehend this! Admit this. Rest here and find old fears vanishing like morning mist before the sunshine.

Our heritage is the life that Isness is. Who could want more? Who needs more? What a delight to discover that this seeing, this hearing, this feeling, this visioning, this listening, this delighting HERE AND NOW is the all and only action of God being God.

What can *happen* to this consciousness, the Life-I-am, the awareness I am? Naught but what can happen to God. And what can happen to Singleness, Omnipotence, Purity, Perfection? Nothing, nothing! I tell you the seeing of these words is God's *eternal* Self-witnessing *in action,* already here, already now. No wait. No struggle. No suffering. No testing or waiting through the pendulum's dark swing in order to find a measure of relief at the other end. The struggle has only to do with the fruitful, but not necessarily easy, task of letting go the old view of oneself as a *possessor* of life, as the grand custodian and *manipulator* of experience.

EXAMPLE

Look outside at the sleeping tree there. Who sees the tree? Bill or Deity? Does a body do the seeing or does *awareness, consciousness, life* see it? What sees the tree? Consciousness? — or a body-centered custodian of consciousness? *Where* is the tree. Fifty-seven feet removed from a body-oriented ego-container of awareness, a judge who likes or dislikes what he sees? — or is the tree *within* awareness? Is the seeing of the tree the *activity* of a separate-from-the-thing-I-see recipient-of-life, a so-many-year-old male or female pump filled organism who looks out through bloodshot eyes and answers to the name of Bill? — or could it be that it is *Deity being the "seeing"*? Indeed, isn't it just possible that Isness, Reality, God, is the seer "seeing" *and being* the seen? Could it just be that "seeing" *itself* is the identity "we" are? Could we be Life *itself* rather than the recipient of it? Indeed we can! We are!

But lordy, lordy, what this does to the old theological concept of a *bestowing* God. What this does to the theological view of a man born in sin, a *recipient* of Life—or to the oft expressed metaphysical view that Self-ignorance, via its own effort, must lift itself up to Wisdom. We awaken to find the great gulf twixt God and man has gone. God is no longer remote. We are no longer a fawning, cringing *recipient* of Life, worshipping a non-existent *Bestower*. This life right here is it. *This* living, *this* seeing, *this* being is the IT which God is *being*. "Closer than breathing," even as the prophet said.

Reader, there is nothing difficult nor abstruse about this view of the universe. We shall all grow into such a view—the world shall—*and it is coming rapidly.* It comes gently and easily if we lower the walls and relinquish the old concept. It comes with a wall-cracking, bud-bursting blast if we insist on continuing with the wall building ego role of yore—a role that may seem personally delightful but has been a near-fiction from the first; a role apparently calculated only to give us the present wherewithal to speak with authority and be effectively about the Father's business of removing the restrictions and tending the New Garden that Now is.

We awaken with joy to find that it really *has* been the Father's pleasure to give the kingdom to us. We find Mind's action of Self-appraisal to be our Identity. Mind knows Itself *as* Itself, and this life we are is that knowing going on!

"Seest thou this?" If so, it is time to "be'est us this" and begin to live the Millenium it is our heritage to be.

RESPONSIBILITY

For a very long time (as time goes) the deep study of Western metaphysics had me feeling guilty for all that appeared "bad" in my experience. The sins of the world were heaped upon my shoulders, because it seemed to me that I was the personal author of all that appeared as my experience. Well, the lights of the world have never *intended* to convey such a sense of personal responsibility.

This consciousness is finally discovered to be *God's* Self-awareness for which God is responsible, and for which "we," *as humans,* have no responsibility whatever. "We" do not have to live "our" Awareness. *God* does. And, despite many, many "absolute" pronouncements to the contrary, the awareness that presently includes these words is not being *all* there is to "God." Rather, *God* is being all there is to this awareness—and there is a vast difference of confusion, wild goose chases and agony between these diametrically opposing (but subtle) viewpoints.

So we gird up our loins to be this NOW-awareness for which God is responsible, not "us" responsible. As "explosion" takes care of the "sound" of the explosion, exactly so, *God's* awareness of all God is *takes care of* "awareness".

To say this again: Awareness, life, is not being all there is to God, but God is being all there is to Awareness —and as awareness, we have nothing of ourselves to *do* except be the faithful witness we are and stop the business of playing the hypnotic role of an independent actor. You see this, I feel it!

Just last week someone told me, "God and God's awareness are a clear duality." Not so! A television set and a television set's *functioning* are not two television sets. The misery of the Absolutist's role we play is the attempt to make the *functioning* into the television set. Individual identity is *not* God. Rather, *God* is *being* Individual Identity. Awareness-I is *not* God, Reality, Isness, etc. Rather, *Isness* is being this here and now awareness I am!

In the words of the illustration: The whole TV set is being its own *functioning,* but the functioning is not being all there is to the set. The *set* is *responsible* for the functioning. God, Isness, Reality, All, is responsible for what *presently* appears at hand, so we do not have to waste our time looking ahead, or "upstream". We buckle up the armor and do not do it.

Instead, we enjoy the picture, the chair, bird-song, child or whatever is *presently* within awareness, knowing Isness, God, is responsible for it all, not an independent, big cheese "me". We let go the "me" and find I.

CHAPTER VII

Simplicity In Reality

Surely, simplicity is the profoundest of the absolutes. Of the thoughts the world has considered, meditated upon, contemplated and pondered at length, none seems so difficult to be comprehended by the metaphysician-philosopher we play, nor more persistently disparaged and denied by our intellectual nature than the ultimate *simplicity* of Reality.

Yet, wherever the Light has been seen, in whatever period or culture, regardless of the former beliefs of those "within whom this Light has bloomed or upon whom it has shone," the words that tell of it invariably speak of its availability, tenderness and transcending simplicity. Enlightenment reveals that the Real appears a mystery only to the sophisticated (dishonest) nature of us, withheld from those who would search for it outside the childlike essence of their own being.

To those who struggle for their divinity in the diverse places conditioned thinking dictates, those bewitching webs of erudition that titillate the personal ego rather than dismiss it, the Light remains forever a mystery. Oh, but it comes, it comes! The Light comes "in good measure, pressed down, shaken together, running over and put into the lap" of those who are willing to let go the vaunted self to act the simple Child of God we are in fact already.

So we see, the Light of the inexpressible demands only the sacrifice of a phantom role we play—but the surrender of anything less is the dream of darkness perpetuated.

(Reader, while this has been written in my words, it is to be read in yours.)

ABOUT READING

As all who study with us at Lollygog know, we suggest that *reading* be done with a tender touch. There is nothing so profound about Reality that we need be carried away with an intellectual struggle attempting to comprehend.

Wisdom is being the same consciousness that reads these words and looks outside the window at the trees moving in the wind. How intellectually profound can one be while looking into the eyes of a child? While smelling the fragrance of a flower? While soaking up the warm sunshine along a trail leading to the river bank? What is this business of analyzing, comparing, evaluating and judging? Why the flood of words to get at Truth when Truth exists without words at all? Why the volumes of hot air and print when words are but symbols of Truth in the first place?

I would tell the struggler to put his books down for a time and go out into the fresh air away from the paved streets and find a new pathway to walk, and there enjoy the now-moment. Let him take the thoughts that come from *that* experience—or the feelings, if no thoughts come —and ponder them for a time, rather than his books.

As we walk, we look about ourselves intently. We look at the large things—the hills, the clouds, the houses and trees. We look at the small things—the flowers, leaves, bugs, puddles, the twists and turns of the pathway and the rivulets fallen twigs make in the stream. Reader, consider all these things as you walk, ride or dream, and consider just *who* says anything about them is *either good or bad!* Ask yourself where judgment enters the picture. So the old barn is about to fall down—is that bad? Wouldn't it be strange if it didn't fall, the way the foundation has rotted away? And is *that* bad? What is wrong with old wood returning to the earth? Who says *anything* is bad? Who says the world is coming to an end? Nothing is ending along this beautiful pathway except the foolish and unnecessary practice of judgment! And shouldn't personal judgment end?—especially when we see how glorious the unjudging view of the world is?

Yes, the turn from the "world" is a turn from judgment, comparison, analyzation and evaluation. The "return" to the Father's house is a return to tender simplicity. Not a remote simplicity, but HERE! Right here, right now! Do you see this?

We end the hassle with words and the struggle to understand. We stop battling with intellectuality for a time. There is only to *be* Awareness in this NOW. The Identity being consciousness is continually "experiencing" the constant awareness of Truth on earth despite all that has been written to the contrary. It is a matter of letting go the judge who does NOT see perfection for making imperfection of it. It is a matter of letting go excessive intellectuality. It is a matter of being *honest* and ending the attempt to be an imposter who judges everything and then reacts to those judgments as if *they* were the Authority.

I would tell those who are weary of the struggle to take off their shoes and walk barefoot in a cool stream. I mean nothing symbolic here. I mean to take your leather shoes off your feet and put your pinkies into a real stream and get sand between the toes the way we did as children —the way we still do as children here at Lollygog.

I would tell the weary to sit right there on the bank and watch the minnows darting upstream— then watch the circles grow from a pebble tossed at a floating leaf. I would say to consider that leaf a moment. It is just a leaf being a leaf. There is peace and tranquillity there. It is not struggling to alter the scene around it. Neither are the reeds nearby. There is no sadness there whether we happen by or not—whether the wind blows or doesn't.

Reader, is this too simple and naive? Intellectuality certainly thinks so—but intellectuality has failed to bring Peace; intellectuality has failed to show us Tranquillity. I tell you that this simple act of naivete, this inane and childish bit of silliness (as judged by the world) will sooth the troubled breast and open the doors of the Heart to arenas the intellect knows nothing about! We do this and *then* find our books saying more to us than ever before.

Well, enough about this. To write or read of it is only that. Oh, but to *DO* it is to return to childlikeness wherein the spirit soars and the Heart sings a new song of zestfulness.

Take a solitary stroll and see for yourself.

THE MAGIC OF A SPECIAL PLACE

We should all have a special place. Let me tell you about mine.

Not far away is a rolling hill, a green pasture now, and down those smooth slopes at the bottom lies a square field, corn and cotton in the Summer, vetch and oats to rekindle the soil in the Winter, surrounded with old, black hardwood posts and rusty wire, wild ivy wrapped around —and honeysuckle, blooming and sweet and droning with bees.

Along the west edge of the field and down to the river stretches a cool forest, not virgin, but many years since it was timbered, filled with shaggybark hickory, pine, scrub oak and those noble sycamores patched with pure white and crowned with thin silver leaves that flutter in the least wind.

My path takes an unnecessary turn from the straight way to pass a special cluster of those soft regals of the woodland. I have a friend among them, an elder statesman that stands a hundred years tall, has seen many an Alabama thunderstorm, and oversees a small opening in the woods marking who knows whose once-upon-a-time patch of melons and greens. If I'm not in a hurry to get down to the river I stop there and sit down and lean back against my sycamore and watch its shadow grow long across the opening while distant birds go soaring in the Summer wind. It is a warm place to dream and turn loose cares and let troubles go winging with the clouds from the south.

Everyone should have such a place when things seem oppressive. Everyone *has* such a place. Maybe not in a patch of wood along a river bank, but mayhap in the Tennessee hills or the mountains of the West, or a backyard garden or the shady corner of a porch. It may be a special chair alongside an apartment window overlooking a glistening wax-leaf privet and walkway grass, untrimmed and bending in the West wind. But wherever, all of us have a "place" wherein thoughts come forth of an especial feeling quite beyond the usual—clean thoughts of wistful grace and gentle uplift like a sycamore—warm, tender and powerful.

These "places" are not mere locations bound about in finiteness and time. Dear reader, I suspect you already know that they are the manifestations of the Heart's Secret Place. They are the products of the Within.

This wondrous place of mine with its guardian sycamore is not bound to a dimensional woodland a few miles away. It is here right now, closer than breathing, closer than fingers and toes, a simple second's silence from seeing and being. It is in the Mind's eye and I may visit it in a twinkling!

Come with me and I will take you there.

ENDING THE STRUGGLE TO UNDERSTAND

"Mr. Samuel, I have been searching for Truth with all my strength, *but* . . ."

The struggle to understand is damning. Excessive effort is anathema to Truth. The very one who strives with might and main to crash the gates of comprehension is the one who will NEVER find the feast within.

Crumbs, mayhap. Here a "healing," there a "demonstration," line upon line, precept upon precept, here a little, there a little, but never Wisdom ITSELF. Never Realization ITSELF. The one who struggles will ever be the struggling one. The one who climbs toward Truth will ever be the climber. The one who grits his teeth, juts his jaw or argues is the metaphysical masochist who beats his head against a wall—a self-constructed wall that exists because he would insist that an ignorant identity is his *present* identity. That pseudo-identity and the wall of ignorance are one.

Listen softly. Listen gently: whatever wig-wagging gyrations the leaf on a tree may perform, it is the *tree* living the leaf and the leaf is nothing of itself. The *tree* is the leaf. The leaf needs naught but to be itself—which it is being already in fact, through no prowess of its own.

Listen again: the bud on the bush, closed within itself in darkness may think it is an identity capable of independent action. It may feel it is blooming itself through its own great effort, but when the bud opens into the light of day it looks 'roundabout with new amazement and declares, "BUSH am I, not bud! BUSH is being all I am. BUSH is this IDENTITY, not bud, not Bill, not Ruby. And bush is being *ALL* I am. As a bud I am nothing of myself, at all, at all! BUSH am I, neither suffering nor afraid."

Reader, do you see this? Do you see the wisdom of letting go? Do you see the stifling, self-perpetuating *arrogance* of viewing oneself as a bud-identity struggling to "break through"? The effort to lift ignorance up to Wisdom merely perpetuates the belief of an identity in need of an uplift. We let go excessive effort. We sit easy. We rest in the already.

My quest for Identity took me many places in the world and I have studied at the feet of many "enlightened" teachers within and without. Each in his own way said the same thing—that "perfection is *already* spread over the whole face of the land but men perceive it not." "I have sought Truth all my life, but lo, that that I seek, I am!" "Not with a mighty effort but with gentleness and grace." "Not by might nor by power, but by my spirit, saith the Lord of hosts."

Dear reader, for whatever it is worth, I tell you that REALITY, PERFECTION, JOY, HARMONY, the *already* Isness that the SUPERNAL is, *is being the present awareness reading these words*. GOD is being the awareness-I-am, this life "we" are. GOD is the responsible one; not you, not me, not us. ISNESS is this AWARENESS being "us" and Isness ALONE is responsible for it.

We begin the break with "mortal mind," the mis-identification, the "old man," "the liar from the beginning" when we admit to the empty nothingness of an ego struggling to comprehend the Truth—and acknowledge the allness, the exclusive ABSOLUTENESS of God. There is nothing unenlightened about the awareness reading these words. All there is to ignorance resides in and as a role we play as a taskmaster of awareness, trying to force it to do the taskmaster's bidding. Only that ignorant taskmaster needs a "breakthrough." But, as bush is being blossom, so God is being this only Identity. We stop playing the struggling idiot to joy as the wisdom Identity is—already!

LIVING THE TRUTH IS NOT LETHARGIC

There is an experience of *direct* Enlightenment that reveals the already harmony, perfection and singleness of God, man and the universe.

Every inclination of the human nature is to continue striving for goals, conditioned as it is to believe it must *do* something to maintain its position.

Every urge within the human breast is to resist the NOW, so it is natural to hear the human charge of lethargy brought down on every statement of an *already* perfection.

Jesus began his ministry with the statement that the kingdom of heaven was already at hand, but there was nothing lethargic about his life. Everyone who begins to examine and *live* these principles will find the experience anything *but* lethargic! See for yourself. New actions, new experiences, new revelations will burst through any fear of lethargy or non-action that you may be harboring still. You will find yourself living a new life of wonder after wonder after wonder. And you will wonder ever after.

CHAPTER VIII

A Practical Philosophy

The world is full of philosophies that are neither practical nor relevant to the daily experience, incapable of being put to practice and their honesty proven. THIS philosophy of ABSOLUTE AWARENESS is eminently practical and immediately provable. It begs to be taken out of the arena of speculation and comparison and *put to the test* that its fruits may become *tangible* in the apparent world of our daily affairs. "*Prove* me now herewith, saith the Lord of hosts, if I will not open you the windows of heaven and pour you out a blessing that there will not be room enough to receive it . . . All nations shall call you blessed, for ye shall be a delightsome land."

Now, for those like myself who have searched for the "something to *DO*" I offer the following which has been helpful. It is only an outline—to be put to use in your own way.

A WAY TO BEGIN THE DAY

First, consider the way an ordinary day begins: One stirs. There is an awakening consciousness of pillow and bed—finite "things." Slowly, one thinks of window, chair,

door, dog, shower, breakfast, coffee—all limited, finite
things. Thought wanders to the coming events of the day:
business, perhaps, or family, or special chores—again limited images, finite forms, events in time.

As you see, thought begins by moving out of quietness
into the arena of people, places and things; out of an
undelineated stillness into the frantic tangle of limitation,
measure, action and reaction. It is as though the conscious
experience were forever heading into increasing numbers;
into multiplicity. We awaken in the morning and, if we
follow the patterns of old, thought moves immediately
into a disorganized world where unexpected actions occur;
where generally unpredictable reactions spawn unexpected consequences and we find ourselves the fallen victims
of finiteness.

Now, reader, consider this beginning day in another
light. We awaken. Again there is a consciousness of pillow
and bed. And again, out of old habit we see the window
to be closed, the door to be opened and think of the
coffee to be started—all finite things. Ah, but *this* time,
right here, right now, we determine to *turn thought in
the other direction,* 180 degrees *away* from the rush
toward finiteness. For a brief time we lie still and consciously bring ourselves to consider single Infinity, the
allness of Isness. We lie still and think of the infinity that
Being is. This time we ponder wholeness, singleness,
completeness, oneness, harmony, perfection.

During these moments we may ask, "How infinite is
Infinity? What can circumscribe Infinity? What can
bind or *limit* Infinity? How all is ALL?" We ask and
answer these questions for ourselves.

We consider the *oneness* of Being. How total it is!
How complete! No limitation here. No finiteness here.
UNBOUND Being being all.

Mayhap we ask, "What is being this consciousness that appears to be lying here and contemplating? BEING, GOD, PERFECTION is being this awareness, isn't it? Indeed. Therefore, PERFECTION is conscious. PERFECTION is awake. Perfection is LIFE, perfectly alive and vital!

What does infinity know of Itself? Is not the *knowing* of unbound Infinity unbound also? Of course. Its unbound, unlimited "knowing" is infinitely operative as *this* consciousness-I-am, right here, right now.

What is wisdom? Is it not Infinity's knowledge of Itself? Deity's SELF-knowledge? This conscious awareness is that knowledge in action! Consciousness, unbound, unlimited, infinite. *This* consciousness presently considering these things is infinite Wisdom in eternal operation.

We ask, "What does Infinity know of Itself?" It knows Its own qualities and characteristics. How? *Specifically* (as well as universally)—each distinctly delineated from all others, the consequent appearing of "form".

So it is, we find the morning's contemplation of Infinity soon leads us to perceive the same "things" as before —home, family, business and affairs; but now these "things" are no longer disorganized obstacles lying in wait to trip us or spring an unexpected disaster. Instead, they are the clearly delineated and discerned qualities and characteristics that Harmony, God, Isness is being—AND THIS LIFE WE ARE IS GOD'S AWARENESS OF IT ALL!

Notice, it is the same morning, the same bed, the same home. It is the same conscious awareness, the same "Identity" *but the views are different.* The old view, out of pure habit and without a thought of Isness, moves immediately into a world of disorganized images primary to it. It moves relentlessly, inexorably toward multiplicity and complexity into an ever proliferating concern with a jungle through which one, if he is to survive, must tread a cautious, defensive path.

But the view that *breaks the old habit* and begins the day with a gentle, happy consideration of a perfect IN-FINITY is like the prodigal's rush to his Father's King-dom—like coming home where the basis for harmony lies; where ISNESS is put first and found to be the ordered substance of "things" and those "things" of per-ception seen in their proper perspective.

This is the view that comes in from the threatening storm of intellectuality and rests with calm assurance in the shelter of Simplicity all the day long—all the day long. This is the view that sees the pitfalls for what they are and does not have to fall in them to learn their lessons. But, if we *should* stumble and fall, this is the view that allows us to be quickly on our way again, blessed by the experience; *blessed* by the experience!

Try this, reader. Try this and *see* what new sparkle it will begin to add to your day. Then, when you have proven it (and you can prove it this very day) tell others!

CHAPTER IX

The Phantom Of Fear

Dear Mary,

Concerning fear, listen with your Heart!

The images on the television screen may appear to shake, jump, roll and crack asunder but their gyrations do not, *cannot,* do anything to the screen. Can they?

Our Identity is the screen of life, "within" which the images of people, things, events, etc., appear, but those events cannot do anything to this Identity we are no matter how much they quake or threaten to!

"Seest thou this?" The consciousness that even now reads these words is the "screen" and the images included within it can do nothing to it or for it.

So do not be frightened. Words are just words; threats are just threats, sights are just sights—all powerless. Power ever resides as *God, Reality, Isness* which is even now *being* this awareness-we-are, this *Life.*

Reality is in no way *self*-destructive. The Identity we are is the very *self* of Deity—and there is no need for fear.

Have we not heard that "love casts out fears"? Have we not also heard that "God is love" and that God is all? Isn't All *all?* To be frightened is to disavow God's exis-

tence—and even a shadow cannot disavow the substance
that produces the shadow. Unless God is frightened of
Himself, fear is illusory—

Well, God is *not* frightened and fear is senseless foolish-
ness, powerless to bind us. We are *not* bound by fear,
Mary, and you do not need to act as though you are.

Dear John,

To the point quickly:

I am aware of your fear and the depth of it. Furthermore, I'm aware of the sundry pictures that present themselves as the causes of fear and how very real they seem.
But I am also aware, whether anyone on this earth believes
me or not, that those appearances do not have the authority *in themselves* to cause us to panic. Our fear, like our
grief, is often self-induced self love—unadulterated selfish-
ness about a separate self that doesn't even exist in Truth.

Does the *real* Identity agonize? Does the *perfect*
Identity run around in a panic? It does not!

Then what does? The insidious possessor of the scene!
The imposter who wants everything to be exactly what *he*
thinks it should be.

Is the *only* Mind in all existence afraid of losing an
aspect of Its own Self-awareness? Is Mind fearful it will
forget something Mind knows Mind to be? *If Mind is
not afraid, who is?*

If you say *you* are, you have the wrong you. *That's*
the one to stop playing the role as.

We do not make progress out of strife. It only seems
that way because the strife (fear, consternation, morbid
depression and grind in the belly) is like a dam that
blocks the flow of Unfoldment within (and as) itself.

When the block is lifted momentarily, the accumulation rushes out into *conscious* awareness. Only that *imposter,* who lives the belief of the block, views his agony as a means of discerning his harmony—though it surely appears to be the only way we can find it so long as we are still struggling to be that unenlightened blockhead striving after a healing.

Right now, right where you are, there is nothing that needs to be healed! The old nature of us believes there are appearances to belie this, but if we are going to *react* to those appearances as if they were an imperfection, then we do not really believe that God is ALL. Do we? How ALL is YOUR all?

Come home to your own "feelings" and insist on the "feel" of equanimity. *In truth, we do not "feel" because of the sights and sounds of awareness; rather, sights and sounds appear as they do "because" of feeling.* Find this sense of peace first. Experience follows suit.

"Son" is an idea included within consciousness. There are no diseased *ideas.* The very one you *tangibly* see, hear, talk to and love is seen (heard, felt) within the consciousness presently reading these words. Consciousness is God's action of Self-perception and God is quite responsible for all it contains and for perceiving it perfectly.

We are consciousness (awareness) *Itself,* not the personal, responsible, demanding *custodian* of it. Our happy awakening begins when we see this gentle fact and begin to end the impossible role of *owner, possessor, director, dictator* of awareness.

We should no more attempt to stop *thinking* than we should attempt to stop the images on the television screen. What appears as much of the metaphysician's present agony is the consequence of such attempts. What do we do instead? We pinpoint the old identity as *director,* and give *that* one the boot. (Imagine how miserable would be the television screen that attempted to direct the images as they come and go. The screen's "salvation" comes with its recognition that its attempts are vainglorious and arrogant, even as is the belief of an identity who could do such a thing.) *Then,* recognition of the *whole television set in its singleness* dawns and the screen lets the *whole* be "responsible."

Dear John, Isness really is perfectly responsible.

Kindest regards from my hills of Alabama,

CONCERNING LONELINESS

This work is a positive end of fear and loneliness. You will see! Awareness lives forever alone as itself and this is not a loneliness. This is not an existence that misses anything. Rather, Awareness includes every person, place and "thing" constituting the tangible universe. We live as solitary awareness and *then* find "experience" chock full of non-loneliness, high adventure and things to do that *preclude* aught but a constant sense of peace. After all, does not consciousness *include* everything within itself? *Every*thing!—from the least sandpiper running through the tall reeds to the Pleiades and every star in every galaxy that exists — from every sound that has ever been heard to every face that has ever been glimpsed. Does it not? It does! It does!

Mary, I have news for you: The Identity that awareness-being-you is discovering is *Self*-satisfied and knows nothing of loneliness. There is not "another" for you to miss. There is naught to feel but Self-satisfaction.

Sit easy and listen softly to the following: "husband," "family" et al appeared as images *within* awareness. Awareness did not put the images there, nor is Awareness responsible for them. Who did? Who *does? Reality, God, Isness, The Ineffable One, The Single, The Only, The All.* And what *are* "images"? That which God knows God to be—the infinite qualities and attributes of Deity.

God *still is* every quality and attribute God ever "was". This is so! This is true! *And the awareness that presently reads these words is God's Self-seeing, still seeing God's Selfhood.* Awareness is not experiencing loneliness!

CHAPTER X

The Parable Of The Blossom And The Vine

Once upon a time, a morning glory blossom bloomed on a fence post. It looked out and gave its view of the surrounding pasture. "This is how things are," it said.

Hanging from the fence's middle rail, a higher blossom on the vine looked out and saw the same pasture but its view was higher and more expansive. "No, *this* is how things are," it said.

But the lower blossom argued, "You have been led astray. You have abandoned the original and fundamental view of things. Furthermore," it said to the higher blossom, "you are talking about things I cannot understand."

Whereupon the bloom hanging from the center rail looked down its lovely petals and averred that from its higher place it could see new things to talk about. "I am in a position to judge the immaturity of your view," it said to the bloom on the bottom. "Quite simply, you are not as absolute as I am and you will never understand my view until you reach my level of comprehension or until you have suffered as much as I have."

Now it happened that at the very top of the fence, a third blossom opened its face to the sunshine, looked about, examined itself and discovered that its real identity was not blossom at all, but *vine;* vine *entire; vine*-being-blossom; vine being every leaf, every winding stem and twisting feeler of the morning glory. In new self-knowledge it declared, "While closed within myself as a bud in darkness, I believed I was a blossom; but now, turned from the dark self to the light, I find Identity vastly more than mere bud. VINE am I, above and below, first and last! These blossoms are ME. It is my SELF I see. The vista of EVERY vision is *included* as this single vine I be."

Needless to say, as we begin *living* the all-inclusive "vine-view" of singleness, oneness, allness, the old, habitual way of looking at things cries out in awful condemnation. It considers an all-inclusive ONENESS something to speculate about, theorize about, talk and argue about, even write about *but not to live*—because, living it excludes the "bud-view" as *either* correct or incorrect. It simply sees the bud view as the bud view, this church's view or that philosophy's view as a view being a view, all a part of the *whole* picture.

It is well to add, we have not really forsaken the bud view of things so long as we attempt to defend the Vine's views by criticism and condemnation of the buds. This is only more of the same self-condemnation. The whole purpose of our study of Truth is to awaken to the futility of such self-condemnation and of our reactions to it. When we do, we find ourselves LIVING a new peace beyond the bud's comprehension.

THE TRUTH ABOUT IDENTITY

WE DO NOT HAVE TO LEARN TRUTH! This is a notion to be discarded. Whether we like it or not, we are learning that we already ARE the Truth.

There is a whale of a difference. Just the knowledge of this fact speeds Self-discovery. How? It has us properly identified. Since I am the Truth, I am not one who is searching FOR the Truth. AS the Truth, I am seeking, finding and becoming aware of the many vistas of my Self-identification. As one attempting to learn the Truth as if it were separate and apart from myself, I am forever falling into the intellectual outhouse of confusion and anguish. Either we will forsake that identification in time or watch ourselves attempt to live its destruction. That one is already swimming in polluted water.

With that in mind, the following statements can be understood easily:

It is not WHAT we read that matters so much as the knowledge of WHO reads; but if WHAT we read tells us *honestly* WHO reads, this is to be preferred to the WHAT that indicates (even by inference) that we are a struggling, imperfect, ignorant mortal identity searching for wisdom.

However, once we *know* who reads, the WHAT can be seen for whatever value it may appear to have, even if it is written from the total absence of a knowledge of WHO really reads.

The literature to be wary of is that which professes to be "absolute" while addressing itself to unawakened mortals. If we cannot find something to read that speaks to the Self as the Self is, then we should get busy and write it—and put it into our own understood language of simple honesty.

We are not struggling to put off the old man. We are about the effortless business of letting go the BELIEF of an old man, a mortal identity. This is to end the belief that beliefs are really going on—and THEN to find ourselves comprehending what "appearances" are.

———

God would be a sadist if one's saving grace depended on a detailed knowledge of philosophy. What kind of god would require continual delving into the abstruse and arcane lore of mysticism or metaphysics as a passport to a Reality that is already ONLY and unchallenged? (Metaphysicians do not call metaphysics "mystical" but virtually everyone else on earth does. Even though we might not call it mysticism, its finer points apparently remain a big mystery to most metaphysicians. "When neither he who speaks nor he who listens has any idea what is being said," said Voltaire, "*that* is metaphysics.")

Reading metaphysical literature can be extremely worthwhile, but it is putting the cart before the horse if one thinks that arduous study is the final door opener to the ultimate wisdom. Academic study is and has ever been the intellect's conditioner—consideration of the bits and pieces of the whole; the measure of the parts; a concern for the relationships of characteristics—and all of this is necessary; all of this is an aspect of Wisdom—but the survey of the Whole and of the transcendent arena which lies above and beyond the fine points of metaphysics (or any other intellectual study) has to do with the HEART, not the processes of mentation. In the "outer" world the philosopher discovers and science rushes to confirm. In the inner world, intellect confirms the Heart's Self-discoveries.

"Then why is the 'enlightened' literature of the world aimed toward the religious mystic and metaphysician?"

Because the "metaphysical-mystical state of mind" (Huxley) is the least likely to slam the door in its face.

By and large, the "introspective self-examination of metaphysics" (James) is most willing to grant the *possibility* of the HEART and its "super-experience of illumination" (Ouspensky).

Ordinary theology is generally unaware of the metaphysical solipsism that undergirds the genuine mysticism and metaphysics whose principle aim is to do more than make a human experience more comfortable. Likewise, the struggle with the detail of metaphysics, as though one were a student, precludes the *conscious* recognition of Identity, the experience usually called "illumination".

This experience is the real aim of genuine "religious" instruction, especially metaphysics and mysticism, but it is not limited to their students. It has nothing to do with intellectual attainment. It has naught to do with who is worthy by any *human* standard, with who has studied what, with whom or how long ago.

Rather, it has to do with GOD—it has to do with deific simplicity and godly gentleness. It has to do with honesty and guilelessness. Most of all it seems to me to have to do with simple, credulous childlikeness, willing to acknowledge the presence of a Light that stands on its own and for which there can be found no intellectual undergirding capable of satisfying the "supreme logic" of intellectualism, nor, I might add, capable of satisfying the monumental ego that the hard study of mysticism, et al, seems capable of producing. The intellect is incapable of opening the Heart. The Heart of the Child opens and intellect follows—filled in a twinkling with an immediate knowledge of detail a lifetime of study could never, never accomplish.

———

Then how do we study? With the gentle grace of Light examining Itself. From the position of Intelligence already intelligent, happily examining and being amazed by its infinite detail. We study by tangibly, practically, actually LIVING the Light of our Self. that has already been disclosed and by ending our reticence to surrender the uttermost farthing of the former (more limited) concept of Self. We study by learning the lessons that come from living our Light enthusiastically—and by telling "others" of the wonders we have found.

But we study best by returning to the native, intuitive, heartfelt Child we are. What Nicoll refers to as the "profundities of paradox" may titillate and inspire us, but the Child we are *understands* them.

Gentle Reader, "I" means IDENTITY, not a suffering, human concept of Self. See these words as your own:

I let go the role of an awakening student. I end the identification of gendered mortal learning this or that. I am not a member of the human race, a one among many, working, striving, struggling, straining, arriving at Truth line upon line, precept upon precept, here a little, there a little.

I am an identity INFINITELY greater, grander than that, and I am not ashamed to say so to my world of appearances even when the charges are that of vaingloriousness and self-deluding insanity.

I take the Divine Awareness of GOD to be "my" identity. I am THAT. THAT is "me" and I do not hesitate to SAY so to whomever may be interested.

Furthermore, I live this identification to the best of my ability, despite the fact this appears to be running upstream, contrary to the world's way of doing things. And I maintain this position to the best of my ability, reminding myself as often as necessary that AWARENESS is the

WHO I am, the WHAT I am, the WHY I am—and
that identity is not a human one, not a worldly one, not
a sick, sinning, ignorant or quarreling one but the HOLY
WHOLE SINGLE ONLY ONE, and THAT am I!

We know what we have found. We know of the inner
peace, the light, love, insight and wonder of Being we
have found Truth to be. The Heart of the one who
reads this *knows* what the Truth has meant over the
years. All the hell-fire and damnation the "world" can
muster cannot efface the Grace we have felt. The chal-
lenges we face, like lions in the Colosseum, may appear to
tear the old nature apart, but all that is torn, or can be,
is a concept that was never real. The Grace of IDENTI-
TY stands untouched, untroubled, singing. . . .

It has been said that the discernment of Identity is an
uphill struggle but it isn't really. We are what we are
whether it is seen or not and the simple knowledge of
this fact is an immense aid in our discernment. Awareness
is our identity and awareness functioning is ever effortless,
ever going about its business of seeing, hearing, feeling
and including thoughts all within itself just as it is
about the business of seeing print on this page at the
moment.

Much of the effort goes out of our daily affairs the
instant we expand our sense of identity from the body-
point from which "things" are observed, to awareness
doing the observing. As this expanded identity the body-
point is not excluded but seen as the central point within
an *infinite* identification that includes all "body-points"
within itself.

This grander identity looks on human intellectuality and knows that it pertains only to the body-point and its relationships with all other images. It sees that the Intelligence beyond intellectuality is its own Self-knowledge of singleness, aloneness, wholeness, oneness. It sees that intellectuality can only know Isness indirectly, via qualities and attributes. But, identified as awareness, we know "God" directly as God's Self-awareness. As awareness, we know as God knows Himself to be. We see with the Eye by which we are seen.

So, we live this "child of God" that we are already, and we live it without effort, without struggle, and most wonderfully, *without inhibitions*. You see, this conscious awareness being "us" is Deity's Self-awareness in action, for which Deity alone is responsible. The weight of the world is lifted from our shoulders the instant we stop trying to be something of ourselves—a human personality, an ego, a phantom big cheese protecting his family from the outspoken teachings of this one or that one, intent on healing Perfection when Perfection stands tall and perfect, quite without need of healing.

To question the wisdom of this utter discard of *personal, ego*-responsibility is the natural reflex of the ego bent on self-preservation at all costs. But, in one way or another, we are finally brought to gird up the loins and LET God be the Alone One on the Scene—even as God really IS the all one. Right here. Right now. Already!

CHAPTER XI

The Illustration Of The Fuzzy Underwear

It was a solemn, dignified gathering of deeply concerned people assembled to learn the Truth. They had gathered, they believed, to hear the final secrets of the universe. At long last they were face to face with the Absolute, the Ulimate, finally, they thought, to hear the gems of wisdom for which prince and pauper have struggled since the beginning of time.

Reader, imagine the dignity of it all; the solemnity; the air of expectancy that filled the room as The Teacher entered. An electrified hush descended. The room became a cathedral. Every eye was upon The Teacher and there were those who thought they saw his aura. There were those who saw angels hovering near.

The Teacher sat down and prepared to speak. The audience leaned forward and with bated breath prepared to catch his every word. Finally after what seemed an interminable time, the Teacher of Righteousness opened his mouth and taught them saying, "Today, this very moment, I am wearing fuzzy underwear."

The honest philosophy, book, institution or "teacher" successfully communicates the Fact that GOD (Isness, Reality, the Ineffable) is the Value, *not the teacher, church or philosophy.*

The *Awareness* that reads these words is the REAL. The images it contains within it are simply images-without-value being images without value, despite their imposing titles and heralded labels. There is no infallible authority "out there". Inevitably, every "teacher" who comes to "instruct" us is seen to be "a little lower than the angels"—that is, without more or less importance than any other experience being this Now-I-am.

"The Teacher" jolted his audience no doubt—the room echoed with dropped teeth and embarrassed chortles—but the statement was no more oblique than many another we have heard. The gentle Galilean's message of pure love included the strong admonition, "He who does not *hate* his mother and father will not be able to be a disciple to me"—meaning, of course, to see images as just images, none to be venerated more nor less than another.

A hard teaching? Not really. The jolt of image-devaluation lasts only for a time before the transcending Love appears wherein everyone and everything is apprehended in grand new Light and our sense of value begins to find the balance.

It seems difficult for teachers and their supporting institutions to be honest in this matter of image value. There is nothing honest about the ego that sees its "others" as ignorance to whom it must impart its much wisdom and learning. Can such a view really be an honest view? Can it tell the image-out-there of its pristine perfection and already-wisdom? It cannot, even though it professes to with much self-righteousness and may even believe it is doing so.

When we start looking up to an out there image as greater than Identity-here-as-Awareness, it might do us well to remember the illustration of the fuzzy underwear. God who lives this Life-here-as-I (Identity) is the primal One. We stop delegating our Divine Authority when we stop giving images an undue value, stop standing in awe before them, and stop yielding ourselves servants to obey them unless we feel the ring of their veracity in *our* Heart. Not the intellect. The Heart.

This does not mean that we stop talking to others, listening to lectures, reading and writing letters or enjoying the beauty of good books. It means that every "Truth" we see or hear is about our very own Being, Identity, Self! Every lecture is about the Single Identity "we" are! While we enjoy the beautiful works of the Lights within Awareness, the truth we are reading or listening to is the story of our own Identity!

CONCERNING THE ROLE OF THE "TEACHER"

The idea has long been prevalent in the "East" and is growing elsewhere that the *only* way to the "release of Enlightenment" (illumination, Satori, Awakening, etc.) is at the hands of a personal teacher. Certainly the teacher, guru, minister, etc. is a grand help, *and to deprive ourselves of their services when they can appear to help would be foolish,* but the belief that one *must* assume the role of a student seated at the feet of a teacher is misleading and defeating.

"Ye shall all know me" is the statement, and the *knowing* that *knows* "Me" is our Identity, already established, at hand, here and now. Ultimately, the Self's Self-communion must be seen to be direct and so practiced.

This does not mean there is not a time when a church, Bible or teacher does not serve a happy, meaningful purpose in our affairs—or that they must all be forsaken when we find they do not have the same relevance the world gives them. The bloom that finds itself separate from the bush and cuts itself away in an act of *intellectual* independence, only finds itself dependent on a vase of water instead, and its petals last no longer than the one on the bush. Genuine enlightenment allows us to see the world *for our own view it is* and without having to contend with it blindly. This is the bloom that does not have to lash out at anything when it discovers its real Identity. Further, this is the bloom that *seeds* and finds its own beauty next season where this season's weeds are a tangle of contradistinction.

AWARENESS INCLUDES ALL SYSTEMS AND TEACHERS

Question: Mr. Samuel, Is it really possible, as you say, to steer a course that encompasses *all philosophic systems* and *all teachers of those systems,* including the "bad" ones?

Yes. How? By viewing systems as we view "images" within Awareness. By viewing teachers and groups as we would view blossoms in a garden—as we would look on a scene outside our study window.

I look outside and see a fence surrounding the pool. If I wished to grow eloquent I could wage a wordy war against "bad" fences which exist, as appearances go, to restrict or prohibit—but they exist as things of beauty, too, and as something for a morning glory to climb. Right now I look outside and simply see a fence being a fence. Any judgmental criticism would be foolish SELF-criticism.

Why would it be *self*-criticism?

Because Awareness and all it includes is who and what *I* am. It is self-criticism as surely as looking at one of my fingers and condemning it for not being a thumb.

If someone *asks* me what I think about fences, it becomes the sensible thing to answer his question. But let my answer be honest! The one who asks is none other than an image within this Awareness-being-Identity—an aspect of the very Identity I am. Condemnation of the fence at this point would compound itself as both an I-like and I-dislike judgment of my own, creating *its* attraction and revulsion with which I would have to contend. Then I would be likely to see the questioner-image having to fight the same battle because of my judgment of the fence. Our stated and written words, therefore, must be as honest *always* as we know how to make them— and it would be best in many instances to limit our conversation to yea, yea, nay, nay, as Jesus advocated.

Now listen carefully. If, in looking out my study window, I see a vagabond hound entrapped within that fence, struggling to be free, and he barks to me telling me of his plight, it would be the wise thing to go and open the fence gate, loosing the mutt and letting him be on his way to explore the universe. But in doing this, I do not have to condemn the fence or tear it down, do I?

"Mr. Samuel, your symbology is beautiful, but what if I look outside my study window and find my son entangled in a briar patch filled with drugs, poison ivy and snakes? If the only way I could free him entailed hacking away at the snakes and briars, wouldn't I hack away?"

Your question is here and now even though the situation you speak of is not. If such a situation presented itself to this here and now, I would do all that appeared necessary to release my son or anyone else—to include hacking at the entangling vines, if this is the only way it seemed I could free my vagabond son. It happens, however, that the judgless view of the universe brings experiences with it that require ever less hacking, attacking, criticizing, condemning, killing or maiming.

The situation you present is hypothetical, you see. Where is any of that going on *here* and *now?* Out there is the fence around the pool just being a fence around the pool and the birds I see inside are not entrapped.

Now, some who come here *appear* entrapped by sundry philosophies which entertain certain ideas as "correct" and exclude other ideas as wrong, bad, evil, etc. These appear to me like fences being fences. People join groups of their own volition ordinarily. Like the vagabond hound yonder, they explore for a time and then travel on to more interesting areas to smell out and enjoy. If they come to us asking for advice while appearing to be entrapped by this or that conditioned thinking, this philosophy or that institution—if they appear to be doing something to their obvious detriment—we do and say what appears to be the HONEST, HONEST release from their predicament. But you see, we do this only for those who come to us asking questions and seeking our help. We are not in the business of getting images to do as we think they should. We are not trying to end the appearances of all conditioned thinking out there. We end our own dishonesty—and find ourselves with ever fewer personal reactions to contend with.

We stop saying this teacher or religion is right and that one is wrong. We view them as flowers in the garden. If a bee comes to us and says he is encumbered by yellow pollen, we would tell him the pollen comes from the sunflowers. Or if the centipede appears to be roasting alive, we would lift him from the hot stone in the sun and place him on the cool earth nearby. But, you see, I would only know how to do this by virtue of the fact that I had had my nose in a sunflower and had walked barefoot on the hot stone myself. I would not hurl invectives at the sun, nor cut down the sunflower.

But that you may be forewarned, let me assure you that your new judgless living will be challenged by the old nature of your world. You will be *accused* of attempting to destroy everything the world considers holy and be sore tempted for the sake of "peace of mind" (for the peace of which mind? The Divine Mind?) to give it all up and revert to the actions of yore. But *"Blessed are ye* when men shall revile you and persecute you and say all manner of evil against you falsely. . ."

For myself, I could not be *totally* certain that living the Light as it was given Me to live was "correct" until it had been lived against every appearance to the contrary, and found to be the superior "way"—the way that has dominion.

It's The Awareness that is Pure, Holy, Sinless, Perfect, Whole and Forever HERE & NOW. The ALWAYS I AM AWARENESS!

CHAPTER XII

The Mirror Of Self

Every teacher, book, writer, practitioner, sage, guru or peanut vendor, by whatever name, title or label he goes, is an aspect of the Awareness (Identity) *"we"* are.

We take the book from the shelf most likely to render a specific service at a given moment. Exactly so, we have appeared to go to the philosophy, teacher, church, friend, stranger or peanut vendor that has unfolded as sufficient for the moment—but that philosophy, teacher, church, friend or stranger is *within* the awareness *we* are. So is the peanut vendor. We are forever looking at our Self.

Now, listen softly:

Just as one goes to the cleanest mirror in the house, the one that is the least distorted and best illuminated, so we turn to that aspect of the SELF that tells it to us "like it is," without mental reservation, without the distortion of personal dirt, without the absence of Light, and for absolutely certain, without making something of ITSELF by belittling others. What is seen "out there" is a mirrored Self-image, but only an IMAGE. The awareness that is the *looking* is the divine, pure and sinless Identity we are.

103

To say this again: The image-form that appears at any given moment is only one of an infinite number of forms that may appear. The value is not in the image. (Nor is the power!) The value is forever in the AWARE-NESS-"you"-are who is the *observing* of the image.

All that could be called Samuel or any other name is only an infinitesimal aspect of the Self's *tangible* declaration—and tangibility is only part of it. There is the intangible That "which is above them all"—the Deific Selfhood which is being all there is to the external tangibility of "form" or to the internal intangibility of imagery.

All that is called the belief and dream of a material existence enters the scene upon the assumption of an identity that limits itself to the body-image. *That* one sees all other images as separate and apart from itself. *That* one calls himself the observer and is continually fighting a battle with his observed. In the sad comedy of proliferating complication that follows, observING (the awareness that resides as the center of it all) goes but barely noticed. However, observing awareness goes on being the Identity we are anyway, whether we are conscious of it or not, and all the trials and tribulations of the limited identity's experience serve to bring us to the consciousness of the *greater* Identity—the one that is real; the one that has never been guilty of ignorance or wrong doing or anything else!

THE PEARL AND THE PRICE

So now you have read these long pages of subtle and deeply involved metaphysical philosophy—words, words, a passel of words. What are you going to *DO* with them?

It would seem they can be enjoyed in either of two directions (or anywhere between)—as words whose ideas are capable of striking a response within, therein verifying themselves—a response to which we then act. Or, (as happens until the grand "turn around" takes place) they can be turned into arcane fuel for that insidiously tenacious game one plays in the attempt to be a smart human becoming a smarter human. Woe is *that* me!

Reader, examine your intentions in all honesty—without self-beguilement—and see if you are finally willing to stop the tinkering with Truth in an attempt to have a happier *human* experience, to honestly surrender everything, everything, *everything* for Its Glory.

Remember that the hidden pearl of great price required that the farmer sell all he had to purchase it. The "all he had" is the price *we* are required to pay—the attempt *to be a human along the road to awakening*. We have never really been such a dream identity, so the price that seems so large only appears that way to the dreamer. The price paid is the blow that awakens him. *Then* it is seen that nothing has been lost (nor gained). Rather, the beguiling attachment to a phantom self-identification is surrendered AND A NEW DIMENSION OF SPECTACULAR LOVE IS *AWAKENED* TO!

But the surrender is made *first* to make room for the Fruit of the Vine.

Then, our cup runneth over!

TRADE IN THE HUMAN ERROR
I.D. for The Pearl.

CHAPTER XIII

Living Allness

Those who study these concepts (without becoming sidetracked in the psychic phenomena that would appear to accompany every devoted incursion into the Real) will find themselves going on to "teach" the Truth. Such studies appear to do certain things in a personal experience, but *this* study *put to practice* brings the "student" to the discovery that he is himself the Light of the World —the healing, comforting Light of Identity the world is searching for. It is not possible to live these principles as they are outlined here without finding oneself a Light that is seen by others—seen in the sparkle of your eyes, in the lightness of your step, in the obvious equanimity and tranquillity you experience when others are flying apart at the seams, disturbed by everything that comes along.

Yes, those who study along this straight, narrow and exclusive line will find themselves becoming "teachers," "writers," "leaders." And, Reader, these services will be sorely needed in the strange agony of world-madness ahead. You will be a pillar of light that leads your own self-concept through the shattering wilderness of world awakening already begun.

If the purpose for your discernment of Truth is self-comfort, it would be best to stay with the applicatory aspects of metaphysics. Personal motives will never allow the *art,* the *living,* the total BEING of Identity to consciously reveal itself to you.

Already many are finding themselves being called on to teach and help others who never thought they would do such things. Many who have studied with me are going on to do all manner of "healing" work, writing and publishing, painting and bringing groups together for study and teaching, things they never dreamed possible for themselves.

So will you if you are earnest in your study of these ideas! But there is nothing unusual about this. It has always been so. You have heard these words before: "All these things that I do shall ye do also. And *greater* things . . ."

The fields *are* ready to harvest. The final crop begs to be gathered and brought into the storehouse before the frost of Winter. Our "awakening" is the world's awakening—and we awaken most dramatically in our helping *others.* This is the way I have been shown and I have been told to tell it.

BUT A WORD OF CAUTION

The corrupting power that a personal following represents can be the bane of the metaphysician who uses that as the measure of his success. The real measure lies in *living* God's Allness as the only Fact of being. The "following" this appears to produce is not likely to be large, but those who find it are the "one in a thousand, two in ten thousand". They are the elect, the chosen of God "whom He hath given us," and we are given all that is necessary. These are the ones who will become the world's grand pillars of strength. And they will each, in turn, be given theirs, and theirs, theirs, all Self-images included in this Awareness I-Identity is.

———————

Dear Mary,

Confusion disappears and order takes its place when we begin our *own* determination of Identity—and stop worrying about what our "others" have to say. Our meditation is most helpful in this regard.

You wrote so gently, "I am trying to really know I am the Truth your book speaks of . . ." Dear one, you do not have to know this in any academic or special way. You *are* it, whether you "know" it or not. *God is all* regardless of our actions—nothing we do or do not do alters the Fact of Reality one iota. Isn't this grand to know?

I have good news for you. If you taught before, you will again—and this time effortlessly. Once we finally come to see, admit and surrender the pseudo-identity we have been enacting to simply *be* the *already awareness we be*, hell breaks loose and exciting things begin to happen —not the least of which is the happy recognition by others of the Light we are. They will pop up from all directions to ask about your happiness, enthusiasm and tranquillity.

You will see, Mary. Mark my words. You will be "teaching" again in the most effective way of all. By being.

———————

As appearances go in the world, storm clouds are gathering, soon to rage across the land and around the earth—clouds of violence and fear. More than ever before it will appear incumbent upon us to be the calm and tranquillity the world so longs to find. We can do it because we are it.

That is, *God* is the Comforter as this unbound Identity-we-are. Ours will be the joy of taking no sides in the struggle and thereby remaining untouched—the pristine mark that "others" may see, attain, and find themselves. This makes us "peacemakers", doesn't it?

Much love,

The practice of *Being* "one-Self" is an experience very much akin to the little roadside buttercup that blooms along the country pathways here. It just "be's" itself and blooms; then each season it looks out on an ever-growing circle of *Itself.* That's what we do. We just "be's" who and what we be—with neither regard nor regret for approval or disapproval.

Ah, but then we are honest in *doing* everything this simple "being" lets us see we *should* do. Most often this is a "telling" of what we have discovered to those who come asking. Mind you, we don't go out proselyting and beating the bushes for believers. We give our pearls to those who come *asking* about our Light. They are the only ones who will listen to the Heart's message anyway. But they will come and we will be faithful to them because "the Father hath sent them to us." Humanity hears our laughter; angels direct the traffic.

What now, Father? I am listening.

There is really no one here but LISTENING.

There is no ego to block; no darkness to stumble in; no agony in the Harmony of the Real.

Isn't the Real here? Where is it if it isn't here? Right here, right now!

Mountain-top Pine

Katheryn Davis
La Crescenta, California

CHAPTER XIV

Tangibles And Intangibles

I look outside my window and see a squirrel scampering up a loblolly pine, bits of bark cascading behind as he goes. In plain terms, that view is "here," "now," "tangible" and "out there" from "Bill". *The entire scene is contained within conscious awareness, however.* The scene *IS* conscious awareness in action. Neither the tree nor the squirrel is separate from the awareness within which they have form and substance. The Identity-I-am is the *awareness* within which the old loblolly and the frisky gray squirrel are befriending one another.

Now I look down and see the arms and feet of one called Bill who is watching the scene. That form is *likewise* included within (as) awareness, but the Identity I *steadfastly* view "me" as (if ever it seems significant to consider the matter of "me") is AWARENESS *and not the body-form named Bill.*

Awareness (life, Life) is the I that I am and never am I *really* contained, bound, restricted nor enslaved by any of the substantial images (forms) that exist within this awareness (or *A*wareness) I am—not even that body-form that goes by "my" name. (*That* form is merely

the point in time and space from which Awareness perceives tangibles.)

Now, Bill goes outside and sits under a tree—something
he is woefully proficient at. (Why do we *act?* Always, we
do whatever seems to be the sensible thing to do at the
moment. And right now, it seems a darned good idea
to go outside and sit in the sunshine.) Two chipmunks
scamper after one another, disdainful of the squirrel. A
little yellow flicker flashes through the scene and stops for
a moment in the hedge. I look down and see Bill's
hands as they write these words. Once again: the Identity-
being-I is *awareness* wherein the forms of chipmunks,
flickers, hands and happiness are discerned. The whole of
Identity is *not* the body-form that appears to be doing
the looking from a point in space. I am AWARENESS,
not *just* the body-named-Bill who writes these words.

This awareness is the warp and woof of every grain
of sand, twig, leaf, pine needle and cone in the INFIN-
ITY that awareness is. In poetic words, I might write that
it truly *has* been "the Father's pleasure to give me the
kingdom" by *being* this consciousness wherein the kingdom is seen, loved, enjoyed and lived.

Generally, this is the solipsistic view with which one
"begins"—but only begins. It is a view that expands,
develops apace "and rises higher and higher from a boundless basis."

It has been my experience that this profound (but
simple) re-identification from the limited body-form called
Bill to illimitable, ceaseless, unchanging awareness IT-
SELF, quickly reveals the singleness and togetherness of
all "things." Then, then—after a common time of personal
self-aggrandizement wherein the temptation comes to
"command these stones" and has us playing at being God,
rearranging the world, all in the name of holy ONE-
NESS, comes the grand Light, the ineffable "awakening,"

the "mystical union" wherein it is clearly revealed that
awareness is the activity of DEITY, the "That which is,"
and it is the "That which is" which is being awareness,
not awareness being the "That which is."

It is known without doubt or equivocation that the
That which is and its Self-awareness-I-am are not two, but
one. "He who has seen me has seen the Father," said
the enlightened carpenter. "My Father and I are one,
but my Father is greater than I. *He* doeth the works. I
bear witness to that which the Father has shown me."
Consciousness (life) is the action of That-which-is. It is
not the volitionally personal, directed action of a recipient-
director of life as the director-created theologies of the
world proclaim. Nor is it all there is to God as proclaimed
by communism, most of existentialism and that portion of
the metaphysical world that writes from the solipsistic
standpoint WITHOUT LETTING GO the old man,
the liar, the mortal sense of self, the would-be *director*
of everyone's affairs.

It is the awful attempt to maintain this ego vaunting
position that PRECLUDES the Union, the Wedding, the
Marriage of Light and Love, the Holy Communion, the
final Light, as the poets, mystics, sages and saints have
rightfully called it. We awaken to the absurdity of preach-
ments and systems evolved from the possessor's position
—from the "this is MY awareness" position.

Notice: This "new" view of Identity does not alter
the scene at hand, you see. The squirrel is still searching
for seed among the pine cones. Awareness still includes
the one called "Bill" with chipmunks scampering at his
feet, but it renders an unbound and eternal Identity free
to soar and sing, free to see and be the living of the Eternal
Light that Love is, enjoying "tangibles" but not *bound*
by them nor encased *within* them.

Humanly speaking, tangibility has to do with the loblolly pine viewed from the body-form's point in space.
That one looks "outside" his concept of self and sees the
tree a measurable distance away. For that one, space is
the measure of distance between distinct images. His
"time" is the measure of movement from one image to
another. Time is valid for the body-image called Bill, but
awareness *itself* "transcends" time in that it has no distance to travel. What can Omnipresence view (and awareness is omnipresent!) that is not already included within
itself? To live as awareness *only* is to find ourselves discovering precisely *what* the appearances of space and time
are—and they are not at all what is generally believed.

"But what of the *intangible* pine?" someone asks.
"What of those great ponderosas that are *not* here even
though I can see them in the mind's eye?"

To the body-leaning-against-the-tree identification, the
ponderosa is an intangible image, within awareness, while
the loblolly "here" is a tangible tree "outside" himself.
Awareness sees both pines *within* itself and recognizes
tangibility as applicable only to the body-leaning-against-
the-tree-position, and *that* only a portion of its province.

While intangibles may be inaccessible dream stuff to
the body-against-the-tree identification, they are neither
dream nor inaccessible to Awareness. The not-here of
space (there) and the not-now of time (past and future)
is the body-against-the-tree's TANGIBLE view of the
infinite Eternal.

There is nothing wrong with the body-view of tangibles
("matter") but it is only half a view. There is the universal (or intangible) view as well. That which is called
"enlightenment" has appeared to me to be a wedding of
the two, yielding quite more—a monumental, transcen-
dental more—than either separately.

Incidentally, the body-against-the-tree-view, being less than the whole view, is all there is to the big human mystery of "gender". If the limited (incomplete) identity must call itself something, it says I am male, or female, and looks outside itself for its completion. We find that only the purview of tangibles is gendered, while awareness in toto is *neither* male nor female, yet being all there is to the appearance of both.

THINGS

What are the "things" we see? They are the tangible (hence, limited) view of the infinite "That which is" or "God". Things are the finite appearing of the qualities and attributes of God. They are that which God knows God to be, viewed by unbound, unlimited, ungendered Awareness, God's Self-consciousness. And that awareness, gentle reader, is the very one you are, right here, right now, reading these words.

Finally, we come to perceive that there is so much more to be seen than the world of images, as those who make this study and live as simple, childlike awareness learn. There is the "Light that is above them all." This Light has *dominion* "over every creeping thing that creepeth upon the earth." That includes this body-form which exists as the "means" by which tangibles are discerned—a body incapable of leading us around by the nose.

So, these things considered, which do we choose to identify as: a sack full of writhing "innards," polluted water and struggling pumps, beset by everything on the face of the earth—or as Love's Awareness, the ineffable Light of Life that has *dominion* over a universe so wonderful that even the body-against-the-loblolly catches glimpses of it in the movement of a tree or the scamper of nature at play?

A little girl stops and asks, "Watcha doin'?" I tell her I'm just sittin' here and loving my chipmunks and my universe. Asks she, "Do you love me, too?" and I answer yes. Then, with very bright eyes and a big, big smile she says, "I love you, too, very much," as she scampers away with my chipmunks.

She scampered with my heart, too, but her gentle smile is here somewhere among these words.

CHAPTER XV

The Balance Of The Heart And Intellect

The recognition of Reality does not *depend* on intellectual prowess. The discovery of Truth *as Truth is* has about as much to do with laborious effort as the closed bud's study of darkness has to do with its blooming. Pride of intellect stands like a dragon before the doors of the Heart, admitting only what it will, and that ordinarily just what nourishes the dragon and agrees with it. Pride grows fat on those bawdy baubles that titillate the ego—those morsels of intellectual profundity that allow the prideful one to judge everything that passes before his gaze, accepting, rejecting, liking, disliking, glorifying and praising or criticizing and condemning.

However, *we do not say that there is no place for the intellect.* Many statements of the "absolute" seem antiintellectual, vehemently so sometimes, but it appears this way only because of our tendency to weigh the intellect so heavily. The world teaches that the Heart is "unscientific," hence, unreliable, and that there is no way to perceive the Truth except by way of "reason" and "logic". Horseradish!

The Heart comes into play with the first bloom of Light, and often with such grand relief that our enthusiasm would toss the "intellect" out of the window. But this is the other extreme. For myself, it seems I have found a happy balance between the two. I have learned to run with the Heart, allowing THAT to temper the intellectual view of things.

This is not quite the world's course. The awakened Heart-we-are does not jump through the intellect's hoop. Nor the world's.

"CHEMICALIZATION"

The upheaval that takes place when one is first introduced to metaphysics is the battle between the heart and the intellect. The battle continues so long as either of these extremes attempts to exclude the other. Intellectuality would exclude the heart; the Heart, when first discovered, would seem to preclude the intellect. Ultimately a balance is struck. Then, this balance *lived*, there soon follows the discovery of That which "transcends" all that appears to be Its own Self-action and Self-explanation.

The Absolute LIVED is cataclysmic! Truth is cataclysmic to a lie. Honesty is cataclysmic to dishonesty. The falling away of the dream is not a matter of *human* happiness any more than the cicada's emergence from its shell is without a sundering, splitting, hellish strain to the shell. But not to *us; only to the shell.*

Enlightenment comes as the breaking away from the shell-like HABIT of mortality.

BY WAY OF ILLUSTRATION

Recall a past habit that you have overcome—perhaps smoking, an itch you were constantly trying to scratch with a cigarette that never quite scratched the itch. When finally it was decided to end the habit, what happened to the itch? *It did not go away until first its demands INCREASED and its bellowing for attention grew louder.* Such is the cataclysmic reaction that comes with enlightenment.

Within the arena of human action, the only way from the itch of habit to the no-itch of freedom is to view oneself *honestly* as the Infinite Identity incapable of itching or being bound. And, certainly, to live this Identity honestly is to *not scratch the itch*—which brings the old habit of personality screaming to be catered to again with new disturbances intended to bring us back to the habit-bound shell of mortality. But be of good cheer, friend— the death rattles of old habit are only temporary. The no-itch, no-scratch Peace just beyond the itch is Eternal!

(The approaching Alabama chigger season has nothing to do with the above selection!)

PEACE OR A SWORD?

Question: Like many others, you have a great deal to say about inner peace. Please explain to me why Jesus said at one time, "My Peace give I unto thee," and at another time, "I am not come to bring peace but a sword." What am I to expect, peace or a sword?

Answer: Consider a great lump of ignorance pierced and sundered by the Light of Wisdom. The lump, split in twain, falls away on either side. It should be apparent that those who insist on the validity of the lump will find the light coming as an awful sword, as a great divider bringing warfare and division. To those intent on a study of the old way as if Truth were somewhere hidden within its enigmas, the falling away appears to be the end of the world, nation divided against nation, two against three in the household, father against son, a destructive turmoil that sunders the customary limits. "I am not come to bring peace, but a sword."

But to those interested in living as the Light—the Light, not the lump—the falling away is seen as naught but a falling away and there is great rejoicing at the *passing of illusion.* "My Peace give I unto thee . . ." This peace looks on the personal affairs of the day without fear or frustration, *knowing what they are and why.* This is the Peace that is beyond understanding, our heritage—our veritable Identity—from the beginning.

THE RETURN OF SENSITIVITY

Dear Mary,

As for being "shocked" by your friend as you mentioned in your letter: The ego persists so long as it is coddled. An actress playing the role of Lady Macbeth—should she become so enthralled with her part that she forgets her real identity—may have to be shocked into an "awakening". In any event, the Truth of Being only appears brutal to the personal sense of self, to which it *is* brutal because it destroys it completely. Jesus said, "I have not come to throw peace upon the world, but fire!"

The "real" Identity (and there is no other) cannot really be disturbed by a rebuking—public, private or otherwise. Identity is Identity. All the hell-fire and damnation this side of the Pleiades will never change Tranquillity *Itself* into non-tranquillity! If ever we are disturbed by *any* sight, sound or feeling it is because we voluntarily play the role of non-tranquillity, believing *that* to be our Identity.

Agony is self-induced, self-acted and self-enjoyed; but this is not the Self we are any more than Lady Macbeth is the actual identity of the actress. Tranquillity (Awareness) itself is the Identity we are, and Tranquillity does not cause itself grief. Is it possible for *all* to be not-all? For Truth to be not-truth? For God to be not-God?

Never! Neither can Tranquillity-am-I ever be "I-am-unhappy."

The instruction of the world appears intended to lift one up to the Light. This work is *comprehended* as a step by step study—here a little, there a little, line upon line, "growing consciousness" of Truth—but it is not a lifting up to the Light at all. It is much more a rapid *stripping* away of the mortal shell, leaving the Real *exposed*. It is an *uncovering* of the Light of Identity which has been here as "us" all the while. It is the *return* of sensitivity in all of its aspects. It is the CHILD uncovered again, stripped of all the intellectual veneers, its worldly vestures ripped away. Without question, this work appears to uncover the Child we are and we stand naked, exposed, defenseless, hyper-sensitive, our perception extremely acute again.

But lo, many, aghast at the old-new sensitivity, pull the covers up again, put the veneer on again. Then, the intellect, by reason of its own ten thousand reasons for wanting to perpetuate itself, attacks that which would make it so vulnerable and exposed. This appears especially true of the ego grown proud of its accomplishments. I have seen many who could stand the pure Light of "reborn" innocence for only the shortest time, thence to return to the blanket heap and greasepaint—and then throw rocks at the mirror of themselves; at those who would "tell it to them as it is."

THE CHILD

I would tell those who have found the Child within, that pure pristine, holy Child you are, to *maintain* your simple credulousness and sensitivity by living your Child-

likeness and Simplicity. Hold this grand awareness close
to the Heart because, in Truth, it *is* the Heart. *Love*
this love you have found yourself to be. See it in everyone
and everything, because the everyone and everything are
but mirrored images of your Self. Do not worry about
Identity being raw and sensitive in the face of the world.
Its defenselessness is its strength. Who would harm a
child? Those who have the courage to remain the newly
revealed Child find that this is so.

And to be the child does not mean forsaking a job or
an organization necessarily, because the Child's view of
those activities is sharp and perceptive. The Child we
are cannot be fooled. We see and enjoy the real, leaving
the rest alone.

Ego shed is Identity discovered.

And this is so!

It is inevitable that there will appear to be the dissolution of all that stands between ourselves and a full knowledge of the Truth. Inasmuch as the world appears to
reside within the awareness-we-are, the dissolution that
began within appears outwardly as the world's search for
freedom and the upheaval it brings. Our inner turmoil
never ends until we reckon Identity as *already* arrived and
then end our attempt to lift an incorrect self-concept up
to the Real.

If we are to see the world scene disclose the underlying,
overlying Harmony "that is even now spread over the
whole face of the land," we must *make* this re-identification in fact and *end* the nonsense of acting out from the
position of a sponge trying to soak up wisdom. To do

what? To steadfastly reckon Self from the standpoint of Perfection. No other view will bring Peace so quickly to the human scene.

LIGHT IS LOVE

The "final days" (and this is all that is significantly meant by those ominous words) is the arrival of the world's final enlightenment. These days are in progress already. The light is dawning because it is already here. New ideas are coming into focus and old landmarks are passing away. Cherished notions, some of them the very pillars of society, are being shaken to the roots. We are finding most of them built on foundations of sand. Many institutions charged with the revelation of God, Truth, Reality, are found not to be giving freedom to their charges but withholding it; not dispensing Light, but darkness; not unbinding men, but shackling them; not seeking out the new Rays of Light and investigating them impartially, but, for conscious or unconscious reasons of self-preservation, doing everything in their power to keep new Light from being seen—for fear, say they, their present Light will be adulterated. As if the Truth needed protecting!

Oh, but let it be understood, these very institutions are a blessing and they are serving a most necessary purpose. How would we know that Identity is Omniscience itself without first attempting to place that omniscience "out there" in a bible or institution or philosophy? How would we learn beyond all doubt that Light itself is being our Identity without first living the futility and impossibility of a weary traveller trying to reach the Light?

So now, to make this statement from still another direction: We come to see the Light which reveals that we *are* the Light. I have found that acting this Identity "on faith" *first* helped disclose the Light-I-am that removes every doubt. And this Light of Self-discovery blooms in illumination and insight—fragile, fragrant, a flowery display of beauty and love divine. Sparks! Enthusiasm! Zest! Strength and youth flooding back! The bloom of Light Divine—the simple Love that is Identity, revealed.

CHAPTER XVI

A Conversation About Guilt

"Mr. Samuel, it seems to me that in the final analysis, the solipsistic metaphysics of the Absolute tells me that I am the cause of the discord on the scene. This means that I am taking on the sins of the world—that I am responsible for every heinous act ever committed that I have ever been aware of. I don't like this at all."

The Christian Christ has been pictured as one who was willing to accept this appearance of guilt, *and then do something about it;* but be that as it may, who says that the expanding view of a society in upheaval is a bad view or a guilty view to be disliked? Who says it is heinous to see our former landmarks being left behind?

We view without judgment because awareness doesn't judge. Society judges. As we look out into the world "tumult," we are merely seeing misconceptions tumbling or not tumbling into the piles of unimportant dust they are. We have seen fit not to continue giving them a power they do not have, but this doesn't mean it is bad or that we are guilty of the sights we see. As awareness, we are not responsible for *any appearing.* Awareness is the seeing of *Deity,* and it is our good pleasure to *be the seeing* that DEITY (ISNESS) is "responsible" for. Just as we come to stop holding others guilty for what it appears they are doing to themselves or society, neither do we hold *ourselves* guilty for being *their* creators. Awareness is no creator. Awareness *beholds* a kingdom which is forever finished. When did "Eternity" *begin?* Really, even the use of the term "finished kingdom" can be misleading. What had no beginning cannot be finished.

"Well, as I understand it, Mr. Samuel, solipsism says that by my act of putting off the old man, the misidentification, I am looking out at my own opposites as they do battle with one another and this appears to be my world in turmoil for which I am guilty!"

Not so! We would like to be the Creator, a Shakespeare who writes and enacts all the wondrous events appearing as history, but as AWARENESS-IDENTITY we cannot take credit for aught. We let the old man bury the old man—and he is certainly doing a thorough job of ending the fiction he began. But that one is not our identity. That one is not awareness. Awareness, here and now perceiving these words, is not guilty of personal judgments or fragmented purviews of Isness without the *knowledge* that they are only fragments.

"But we must put away the former concepts and it is this action that appears to be my world in turmoil and isn't this the most awful guilt of all?"

Listen carefully: The events of history as they are apparently unfolding in the arena of tangibility are *both* (1) the human dream ending and (2) perfect ISNESS disclosing Itself to Itself. The sights and sounds on an historic scale would be appearing whether we were engaged in this *study* or not. Events in the world will continue to go on unfolding as the appearances of people reacting to human pendulum swings one way or the other, but as *WE* put off the *belief* of misidentification, we are able to perceive events as they *are* and for what they *represent.* Furthermore, we are able to stop being personal reactors and become "passers-by." If events are the appearing of a personal dream ending, the *dreamer* is their cause and has the same control as the dream-identity *in the dream* has over the events of the dream. On the other hand, events that are the Divine Isness unfolding to Itself are "going on" regardless of a dreamer's personal actions (or reactions) and his awakening appears as an ability to endure the events without judgment, without blinding involvement and without being disturbed.

"Now I see. All that has been accomplished by becoming so intellectually involved is that now I *know* why 'all things work together for good to them that love God.' "

Yes, and we can see that the appearance of a human awakening going on is only half the scene, for which we are *not guilty!* There is a greater Scene being all scenes.

A LETTER CONCERNING GUILT AND FORGIVENESS

Listen with the Heart, John:

Considering the human scene alone, the "wages of sin is death."

"Sin" is "guilt". Semanticists can rationalize until hell freezes over, but "sin" still winds up being "guilt" — and guilt, sin. Their *"effect"* appears to grind the spirit and body to dust—and "death".

The seekers of Truth finally wind up facing the greatest guilt of all—the most heinous "sin" imaginable: What is it? The belief that, since nothing is external to awareness, then one is guilty of every botched appearance in his world—guilty of wars, pestilences, murders, governments, pollution, over-population—to infinity.

Notice, I just said *facing* this greatest guilt of all—not guilty of it. In this particular aspect of experience (or "cycle" if you want to call it that) it is imperative to see the absurdity of this "final" onslaught of the old nature. It is the "equal and opposite" claim of the same ego which earlier *tries to be God,* using the same pretense— i.e., that everything is included WITHIN me! — that "me" still the old imposter.

This particular aspect of guilt presents itself via any avenue it is given to enter—it says many things: "My life is a failure—I am ignorant—my family doesn't love me— my friends are leaving—I have hurt this one or that one— I have broken up this or that. . . ." — all of which is only the other end of the playing-at-being-God swing of the pendulum.

THE EXTENT OF GUILT

The extent of mortal guilt—that is, the belief and *acceptance* of it—is horrendous. The pressures of guilt are used in every way—even to teaching—even in our casual conversations. Indeed, guilt is the veritable *food* of the "old man." (EGO)

The lids that are popping off throughout the world are mankind's attempts to find an escape from the constant pressures of imposed and accepted guilt. Why, even the television commercials teach, sell, make their points by way of *adding* to our guilt: "Why aren't *you* wearing your seat belt?" — "Are *you* giving your family orange juice every day?"

The body appears to break down in our attempts (subconscious) to justify the guilt we accept from every hand and ultimate "death" appears the consequence.

There is no guilt outside the *acceptance* of it! God is not guilty of doing God in. There is no Identity but the One and that One is not guilty. Guilt exists in the superimposed ego-world which has already served its purpose for you. (Its purpose is to bring us to perceive the ONE and to "learn" *via its contradistinctions* just what the One *is*.) The ONE *is not* guilty of sin, sickness or death. The One is not lethargic. The One does not need to be boosted by bourbon nor propped by pills—and does not develop a dependency on them. The guilt that would tear the body apart is the final "is not"—and *now* you do not *need* more contradistinctions to battle with.

So what to do? Look in the mirror and see that one INNOCENT. Look in the mirror and FORGIVE that one of everything. You can do it because that one is not guilty. That one has never had a mind of its own except in its own belief. But "belief" is just belief—a powerless notion, incapable of doing anything to anything. What can two plus two equals *five* do to the perfect *principle* of arithmetic? What can "is not an oak tree" do to the pine tree? Not a blamed thing, and you know it! A lie is a zero. A big lie is the same zero. A belief in guilt is a zero, incapable of bundling up the nerves, incapable of preventing AWARENESS from doing whatever it seems sensible to do.

Do you understand this?

You *can,* in the twinkling of an eye—and find the RELEASE, the PEACE that letting go the burden of guilt will bring.

We *do* "forgive sins"—by "forgiving" guilt—and you will find yourself quite able to take up your bed and walk wherever you want to!

Walk straight to the mirror first and forgive yourself. Thank the Ineffable HERENESS for its forgiveness of guilt by its *preclusion* of guilt.

... then, watch what happens in the minutes, days, weeks ahead!

Dear John,

This letter comes as a simple "proof" that you have not been forsaken—a few words from me and my pines on this side of the hill.

A grand harmony reigns. While the humanist declares there is no God but mankind himself, I know better. What I have found exists above and beyond the concepts of people. Its articulation, however, is apparently limited. to human words and human philosophic attempts.

> We are not guilty of ignorance. We are not guilty of having created our trials and tribulations. While it seems so—and much of the religious education of the world hangs this albatross around our neck—" 'tain't true, 'tain't so!" The dreamer dreams because the dreamer *is* the dream. To say that the dreamer is responsible for the dream is the subtle birth of guilt—a pseudo-guilt that has never been justified. We are not guilty of a botched experience because of our failure to "know the Truth" or to be honest or any other such thing. *Every "trial and tribulation" of personal experience has worked to prove our uprightness to us*—all events of a natural, normal and happy, happy *awakening*. That awakening is even now going on, and you are my opportunity to tell myself so—even as I am yourself telling you.

All is well because *All* is.

IT IS NOT ENOUGH TO SAY "THERE IS NO GUILT"

There is more to having done with the appearances of "guilt" than simply saying there isn't any. There is even more to it than understanding that there is no guilt. It is not enough to declare with grand metaphysical flourish that "guilt implies sin and a sinner, which are impossible because God is ALL." Oh yes, this is true—God is ALL and this holy ALLness precludes the guilt of wrongdoing —but until such time as we stop *enacting* the role of a guilty sinner by virtue of believing ourselves to be a sinner, then *that identification is stuck with the appearances of its beliefs*—the sense of guilt being the most unbearable, hence paradoxically most likely to shake us from the belief of the imposter.

In short, the appearances of guilt remain on the scene until we stop holding ourselves *or anyone else* guilty. Of what? Of anything short of the absolute perfection they are!

It is one thing to say there is no guilt. It is another to ACT in accord.

There is a monumental joy to be discovered when we release others from any obligation we think they owe us. I did not find myself "free" until I first freed others of any responsibility for my own happiness; until I stopped expecting them to conform to patterns I or humanity had established as proper, normal, correct, polite, expected, etc. I simply let all this go upon discerning the light: in the words of Jesus ". . . forgive us our debts as *we forgive* our debtors."

Of course, this does not mean that we become remiss in what appears to be our responsibility toward others.

Dear Mary,

Listen to these words of hope: From out the depths of depression and feeling of guilt, from out the sense of personal worthlessness, hopelessness, helplessness and despair; from out this nearly unendurable darkness seemingly void of Love *always comes the birth of the Christ Truth within! Always! Without fail! Inevitably!*

GUILT AND IDENTITY

Thank you for your letter which I hasten to answer. The very fact that you are concerned enough to be "seeking" is enough for me to tell you—and very positively—that you shall *find* every answer to the "enigma of life." For a time, they will appear to come to you from books, classes, tapes, conversations with others and letters such as this, but I assure you that each and every one is coming from within your own Selfhood; from your own desire to know the Truth you be.

In the play, Lady Macbeth feels a great sense of hopelessness and guilt for having killed the king. You will remember that she tries to wash the blood from her hands and fails. For one to believe *any* feeling of guilt *to be real* (no matter *what* the supposed cause) may be compared to an actress playing the role of Lady Macbeth *and completely forgetting her real identity*. Her *true* Identity is not a guilt-ridden Lady Macbeth, but a happy and devoted actress.

We have a greater Identity too. Aware of this fact, we are able to go on playing whatever role seems to be our part on the human stage, ever mindful that "things are not as they appear." Let us *leave* "guilt" with the "old man" *whom we are not.*

On the stage, no matter how heinous the sin, it has nothing to do with the genuine Identity. "Though your sins be as scarlet, they shall be as white as snow; though they be red like crimson, they shall be as wool."

Oh, but we remain wary, wary not to use this as an excuse to condone our own dishonesty or to attack the appearances of dishonesty in others.

ISNESS IS THE VALUE AND THE POWER

An all-pervading Reality exists everywhere, being everything. The charging horseman with raised sword only thunders across a powerless stage. The blood he seeks and mayhap draws is but the enactment of a line or two of fiction, a parody on Truth.

On the stage we walk wherever seems best and say the line that reveals the play's harmless beauty—but we remain steadfastly aware that Truth and its enactment are already one and inseparable; that the Reality of God is the Value and possesses the Power.

The Light that Love is lets us see the scene as an undisturbing event that best suits the moment. And what is the moment? Another aspect of Reality's Love coming to light!

CHAPTER XVII

Childlikeness And Love

We let go that proud "I am me," to be Deity's un-encumbered Identity—awareness, childlike witness of Infinity.

Humility has all to do with NOT being the separate selfhood, the old man, the ego, the personality. To let that one go is not to lose the Identity, but to find it. It is not a position of weakness but bedrock Omnipotence itself. And all one need do to find that this is true is to *unmask* the pompous liar and let it go.

The sundry religious systems (even the "absolute" ones) are very strong on correcting the liar's lies but woefully weak about lowering the boom on the liar himself whose role we try so hard to play. Systems intended to *arrive* at what cannot be arrived at are the liar's own creation, not designed to do him in, but very well geared to do battle with what will. The applicatory systems of society apply themselves to everything short of pinpointing that false identification, the *applicator.* We stop being *that* one to be the Child that God is.

Whenever we have had a "glimpse" of the Real, we have come back to *childlikeness* for the briefest moment. To change the glimpse into the Light of the noonday sun, it is only necessary to come back to childlikeness *and stay there, living* the glimpses that childlikeness makes possible.

And what is "childlikeness"?
Simple honesty.
With whom?
Oneself!

Dear Mary,

If you have not already sensed a new Christ-Experience-within, you *will!* There is no doubt. The giving up in total helplessness is the humble act of letting go "the old man": the "sacrifice" of the pseudo-identity. From that moment one begins to discover the mysteries of his Genuine Identity! Anticipate and joy in this happy experience!

As you have heard many times before, God *really is all!* God is the total of all Being and all Existence. God is the *only Identity.* Do you feel that you are *another* identity who must do something (or *not* do something) to be worthy of being who and what you are? God, single, alone and *All,* is the only Identity in existence. God certainly does not have to do something to feel "a reason for living"—neither must *this* consciousness of existence reading these words. This "consciousness of existence" you are is *God's* consciousness *for which God is responsible.* It is not the personal possession of Mary's. All fear and all sense of the absence of Love stem from the single *false notion* that God is *not* all; that there is God and a personal "me" too. Let go the "me." That one is the "liar from the beginning."

And about Love: Our very Identity is Love *Itself.* Love is who and what we *are;* not something we must *do* for others or others for us. The rose does not have to do a thing in order to be what it is. Exactly so, *Love Itself is this Identity.*

Sincerely,

CHRISTMAS IS THE CHILD I AM

The Christmas Season is more than the matter of a few days. Christmas is the Heart's Season and the Heart is forever. Christmas is Love's Season and Love is without end. Christmas is the season that belongs to children and there is no time when we are not children.

What is meant by the Christmas Story of "the coming of the Christ"? The Christ is the Truth. The Truth is the Christ. Truth "comes" as a dawning. The Christ is our discovery of the Truth we *are.* The yearned-for Messiah is none other than the here and now awareness awakened to the meaning of these words. Does not the Christ say, "I *am* the truth"? We declare without doubt or hesitation that we are the Presence of the living Comforter come to "set all things straight." We take this Identity unto the Self and live it. We gird up the loins and *live* it.

Somewhere along the line comes the truthful (Christ-full) discovery that we are not a finite body containing life, awareness, within it, but that we are awareness, Life, Love, containing all bodies within "us." Reader, for me that awakening is the Christmas of the Christ-I-am—a pure and pristine Light out of a new day, immaculately conceived, untouched by the world—a holy Child born in a manger. But a child beset quickly by the intellectual Herod I fancied myself to be.

The child we are survives, however. The child of Light "grows strong" and dares, with simple honesty and actions that coincide, to challenge the fiction for the

fraud it is. This is *your* Season, Reader. This season
commemorates your Self-discovery. This Christmas is
YOU. The pealing bells, the carols, the holly leaves, the
laughter, red noses, plum pudding, tinsel and happy tears
are yours. These things, every one, are ours. They are
us. They are Identity. This holy season is the merriment
that Love is and it commemorates our own Identity discovered.

The discovery may seem to do with time, but the Discovered and the Discoverer are eternal, quite beyond the
clock, above the measure of months, more than can be
circumscribed by strings of twinkling lights or the jingle
of bells. Love is the measure of this Season. Love tells
its story. Unbound, honest, simple, gentle and childlike
LOVE is the gift we open and the gift we are.

THE GIFT

At this moment it seems to me that we have a most important "mission." It is to discover and live the Christ-
Love we are that we may be found to be the comforter
of this world of images that appears within the Selfhood
that Awareness is. "As I be lifted up," says the Chirst, "all
mankind shall be lifted likewise and drawn unto Me."
We give the gift of Childlikeness to our world. We give
the gift of unbounded joy. We give the gift of tenderness
that warms the Heart and brings the soft breath of happiness, the tender touch and the unrestrained tear of grati-
tude.

We tell the story of Identity. We tell the weary who
they are. We show them the Kingdom of their heritage.
We hand them their scepter and point to the limitless
Light of Love which is their dominion. We look up and
out and "show unto mankind his *uprightness.*"

This is the Father's business, so let us be at it.

Dear Mary and John,

Happy Christmas to you folks! This Christmas Season finds a New Star in the Heavens—this one to tell those with ears to hear of the New Jerusalem wherein there is neither sorrow nor darkness, nor age nor death.

The Holy City is *already* the fact, you know. *Isness* is the totality of all Being within which there is nothing that makes a lie. In all singleness there is nothing to make it dual, and we do not have to *wait* to see this fact! While there presently appear to be an inside and an outside, a here and a not-here, a now and a not-now, all these things are only aspects of the Whole, the All—for which this Awareness "we" are is the activity.

Mind (1) aware (2) of Itself (3) is a Holy Trinity to Itself. "Itself" knows these three are One Mind, one Love.

Well, this started out to be a simple Christmas greeting.

Don't you forget that all the carols and bright lights, decorations and happy children are for *you!* Who *else* is the Christ?

WE COME HOME TO CHILDLIKENESS

The Christmas Season commemorates our own awakening, birth of the Christ Truth within, arrival of our own Identity. The Christmas Season marks the prodigal's return from the land of husks. This is the time when the fires of the hearth are rekindled—the time for coming home.

Coming home to what? To consciousness, to Identity, to the heritage promised us from the beginning, to the Love we are, to the carefree Child we are, to warmth and tenderness, simplicity and gentleness—to the *happiness* that REALITY is!

Reader, if I could give you the gift of childlikeness, I would. But this is our nature already—and this is the only nature that comes to see, accept *and live* the Real. Intellectuality decries the season, anxious to explain it and then to have it over. But childlikeness sees the sparkle of silver tassels all year. Childlikeness listens to the laughter of angels every minute. Childlikeness tastes the sweet sugarplums of Simplicity right here, right now— and feels the gentle Love of Christmas forever!

———————

It comes to me to tell you again of the wonders of childlikeness. To simply be Awareness *itself,* letting go the imposter who professes to contain it within himself, we find ourselves "becoming again as children" in thought and deed, "physically" as well as spiritually!

As children none of us were bothered with stiffness. As children our fingers were nimble and without pain. We tumbled in the high grass with carefree abandon and we were barely conscious of a tag-along body. Was this not so? Well, I tell you we are children now. This instant we are the same unencumbered Identity we were then. This moment the gentle Presence that reads these words is *God's* awareness of God—without restraints, without restrictions, like a child.

———————

Indeed, this book *is* yours. The awareness that reads it is the action that has written it.

You will find, if you have not already, the honest study of Truth appears as youthfulness and enthusiasm, as jolly belly-laughing humor, as love and unpretentious childlikeness. Why not? The Gentle Presence is *already* the *finished* fact of existence. It is our happy activity to come home from the aging wilderness of intellectual folderol by awakening to the facts of such a wilderness's impossibility. Where are the unhappy shadows in the sunlight? Where is the Child if not here as the awareness that reads these words?

If God sung the song "Me and My Shadow", who would applaud?

CHAPTER XVIII

Time And Prophecy In The Light Of Awareness

"Is it possible to know the future?"

Yes.

"Doesn't this mean that the future exists?"

Yes.

"How can this be so when the NOW is all we are concerned with?"

Because the NOW is being all there is to *both* past and future. It *includes* all that is called the future, consequently we are enabled to know it; this future we "know" is NOW, not afar off. Only to the conceptual, judgmental way of looking at things does it appear to be not-now and something distant.

TIME IS A MEASURE OF TANGIBILITY

Time is applicable only as a measure between the people, places and things of the *tangible* universe. The absolutists are correct when they state that Infinity exists as a dimension "above and beyond" time. It is beyond time in the same way that the sphere is "beyond" the plane. It does not *exclude* the plane, however. Rather, an infinity of planes constitutes its being, and to be the sphere is to find oneself knowing all about the planes. We would not say, "There are no planes." Instead, we would see them in a new, expanded light. And so it is that unbound, uninhibited Awareness perceives *time* in a new light. This new light, as the prophets of old knew, is the basis for all that constitutes "prophecy" as it *really* is—not as we read about it in the newspapers nor as it has been popularized.

To toss out everything pertaining to "time" as "not absolute enough" is a stage we all go through in our study of Truth, but when we begin to find ourselves knowing certain things that "are going" to happen, we are then looking on time from a grander dimension, not merely disclaiming its reality. The Hebrews of old considered this to be the only legitimate mark of spiritual attainment.

Dear John,

The prophecy "talk" was more novelty than Light, even though everything "happened" exactly so. I have stopped being surprised by such events. There is nothing unusual about what the world calls prophecy, as the ancient Hebrews knew, but what prophecy is, and what the world thinks it is, are two different things. That which it has been my delight to discover and *be* has to do with "broadening and rising higher and higher from a boundless basis." I simply find myself knowing what will "happen" and it is as simple as that.

My morning-glories are deeper blue this year—and climbing higher.

Dear Steve,

If you were here (and in truth you are) I would have you comprehend and experience the singular authority of the following *Action.*

Like the kids of this day and age are begging, we stick to the sights, sounds and equanimity of this *Now,* as difficult as it may seem to be. We simply refuse to go wandering in the far country of a human past or future. The Now is now—and Now is the transcendent basis for all the judge would *call* his past or his future.

We give the lightest touch to plans and calculations. The old nature of us would have us dwell in doubt, confusion and great consternation about the "future." It would even rename that future and call it "My Future-Now-Awareness" in order to go on planning, calculating and worrying about events to come—events that are not now.

The now-awareness that presently reads these words is all right! The awareness that presently includes whatever images are at hand—chair, room, book, window, picture, tree, cloud, birdsong, whatever—is the Now which is quite all right this instant. We remain right here "to be passersby." In and as this passerby we find this Now-Awareness living *Itself as us* and it is not a "we" who are living the Now. We end the "me" who says "my awareness" to simply be Awareness. *Then,* the time-bound me out of the way, we find ourselves knowing many things about the me's "future," and what he calls "prophecy." Chief among these discoveries is the knowledge that the Transcendent Now is *being* all there is to what is called time. As the Bible puts it, ". . . that which is to be hath already been . . . that which hath been is now."

CHAPTER XIX

Contradistinction And Appearances

The religions of the Western world appear to know nothing whatever of the principle of contradistinction. And the grand mystery is, without a knowledge of this "principle," the world's philosophies make virtually no sense whatever. World religion founders for its failure to perceive the point or effectively communicate it if it *does* see it. There are those like Aldous Huxley who wonder if the point was *ever* understood beyond the apparent originator of the religion or philosophy. Of all the followers of Jesus, only John gives clear indication of understanding this profoundly simple but simply profounding aspect of mentation. Of the present religions in the West, only the metaphysical philosophies have made mention of it—and then, only by a handful of teachers who, apparently because of it, find themselves running afoul of everybody and everything relating to their organization or society until they are branded as heretics and condemned as false prophets.

What *is* "the principle of contradistinction"? It is the comprehension of *why* the appearance of things "material," tangible, human—and yet, like the Teh of Tao, it defies comprehension by the reasoning mind of intellec-

tual man. It seems that the hem of this simple, holy
Principle can be touched only by those who are willing
to let go their personal sense of identification; by those
who surrender *all* within their thought and action that
refuses to grant the *allness* of Tao, Isness, Yud, Deity,
Light, Love, Truth or whatever means "God" to that one.

Oh, but the Heart of us *can* understand this principle
of contradistinction and then it can be made applicable
to our daily affairs in such ways as to be astounding!
"And after you have found," said the Carpenter of Love,
"you will be amazed. And after you have been amazed,
you will be troubled." In addition, you are likely to be
ossified, ostracized, excoriated and excommunicated by all
society—not to mention the likelihood of having the tar
beaten out of you, drawn, quartered and crucified by someone (very likely near and dear) in their sincere but futile
attempt to shore-up a loved landmark *they* feel you are
threatening.

But, "After you have been troubled," the gentle Galilean goes on to say, *"you will marvel and reign over the
all."* And you will, if you are willing to stand the gaff!

Ultimately, we find the world's gaff in the side (when
we insist on standing steadfast) is considerably more blow
than go—puff, guff, bluff, without the least bit of *real*
power. Power ever resides here as Identity, not out there
with the images included within awareness—even when
those images appear to threaten body, purse strings, home,
society, family or world.

In the direct language of Laotse, we hear him say: "The
concept of Yin (the principle of contradistinction) is
ever present. It is the Mystic Female from whom the
heavens and the earth originate, constantly, continuously,
enduring always. *Use her!*"

CONTRADISTINCTION IN THE GARDEN

As appearances go, the garden in my backyard requires clods of earth, leaves grown brown, ungainly stems and, sometimes, even thorns in order to bloom the blossoms. Those blossoms appear only lovelier in contradistinction to all else.

When I walk through that garden I see the flowers, not the dead leaves; my Ruby picks a blossom for her hair, not a barren stem; the hummingbird takes his nectar from the bloom, not the thorn. It is a hungry butterfly that avoids the garden just because of the clods.

CONTRADISTINCTION REVEALS FORM

Tangibility requires contradistinction. Who can see a white bear standing on an iceberg in the midst of a snowstorm? The varying intensities of light, be they called color, shading or *shadow,* serve, if nothing else, to make *form* apparent. A new measure of peace is discovered when we grow to see that shadows serve a purpose and are not evil.

Infinite Awareness (Intelligence, Wisdom) is not *limited.* The unenlightened absolutist's dictum that only what IS can be known is a happy notion to latch onto for a time, but it is finally found to be a half-truth that would (if it could) preclude the *infinity* of wisdom which certainly includes the perception of form and a positive knowledge of what "matter" *is.* The "form" of the "tree" is made apparent (tangible) by Wisdom's knowledge that the tree *is not* the meadow, *is not* the hillside, *is not* the sky or any OTHER form but THAT form. Wisdom knows that the tangible "hand" is not the intangible "foot."

The superimposition of the "world" with its agony intrudes with the personal attachment of *values* to the

forms and the contradistinctions that make them tangible.
"This is good, that is bad; I want, I don't want; I like,
I hate; good and evil; real and unreal" — THESE are
the chains that appear to bind; THESE are the chains
that expanding awareness discerns by the uncomfortable
contradistinctions that make them apparent, and make
apparent in order to be loosed and let go upon the lesson
learned. *This* is what is being demanded of us at this
moment of lifting, soaring, moon-landing Self-awareness
which, like the cicada on yon loblolly pine, having lifted
itself from the darkness of the earth now lets go the shell
of a lesser identity. Soon it flies in the Light and sings,
only the empty husk split in travail.

INFINITE WISDOM IS INFINITELY WISE

How *else* but by contradistinction can infinite knowing
KNOW what isness IS? Listen, listen: a child may LIVE
"childlikeness," but the child does not *know* what "childlikeness" is until, by contradistinction, he has lived the
adulthood that childlikeness *is not*. As only the former
pauper can really joy in unexpected riches, so *unbound*
Knowing (omniscience) lives its childlikeness again but
this time *knows* what it is and sings the uninhibited Song
of Love.

QUESTION: How could it be that there was a time
when Omniscience did not understand its eternal childlikeness?

ANSWER: There is not nor was not such a time. There
is only the tangible half of Omniscience pointing out
(identifying) its other half. Eternal, timeless, formless
Isness has no way to appear in form to Itself except as
a sequence of tangible (known) events, that sequence

appearing as progressive "order" and "time" moving in one apparent direction. The physical sciences are just awakening to this fact long known by the intuitive Child we are.

The world is not something to be overcome in the sense of sanctimoniously trying to change everything. It is something to be understood, appreciated and lived to the fullest. This is the action we are engaged in at the moment, reader. This is what we are doing in the study of these ideas—and the reward for the doing is New Light wherein an eternal Perfection already at hand reveals another aspect of IDENTITY, the Alone Self-hood that ALL is—Grand Holy Infinity which is I—and which is being all images, tangible or intangible.

THE CONTRADISTINCTION CALLED DEATH

An understanding of the "principle of contradistinc-tion" allows for the unraveling of a number of mysteries and the tying together of loose ends of metaphysical truth. While our understanding of this principle is not a pre-requisite for arrival, it helps us comprehend why we are already there. Also, it is a means by which the enigma of "death" can be comprehended "this side of the grave." So I will use it in the following discussion of Life's con-tradistinction, called "death."

When we see the corn pulled in the Fall and watch the stalks turn brown in the Winter wind, we do not think of the death of "corn." Rather, we consider corn in its *totality* and know that Winter is not the time of growing. When Summer comes we see the corn standing tall again in the sunshine, swaying in an August wind. It is corn from the harvest of the year before that is still growing green—in another row, perhaps; in another corner of the field.

So, what is this matter of "death"? What is the much ado over it? Why is it an "enemy"? We end the enemy by no longer judging it *to be* an enemy. We end the appearances of certain other things by ending the *judgments* that called those appearances *bad.*

The statement "the last enemy to be destroyed" labels the appearance as an enemy. But listen, listen: it is one thing to see the valuelessness and powerlessness of death and call it a dream. It is quite another to *look* on the *event* and *see* it as *neither* enemy nor friend.

When we stop limiting awareness to just the *tangible* purview of Eternity and admit to the possibility of the *intangible* (as the other half), we no longer see things as beginning and ending, as having birth and death.

In the Winter when the kernel of corn is stored in a bag in the seed house, the full being of corn is there yet. Tangibly speaking, it is in miniature, compared to the Summer way of looking at corn, but it is all there. If we had an internal way, a Winter way of introspectively looking within the kernel, we would find the corn right there as before, without having come to an end.

In much the same way, the human view of existence is a half-view, an incomplete, male or female view, a rich or poor, right or wrong, good or evil, dead or alive view— but a *half view* nonetheless; only a partial view. Uninhibited, unlimited, unbound awareness is a *complete* view, a *whole* view, a Winter and Summer view combined. Awareness views "as a tree in paradise wherein the leaves do not fall in Winter or Summer." (Thomas)

There seems to be an internal and external view of the kernel of corn—a Summer and Winter view. Humanity is geared to the Summer view exclusively—the external view, the good-bad, male-female, real-unreal, relative-absolute, dead or alive perspective.

There is another perspective: the whole view, the centered view, the transcendent view. This is the perspective of uninhibited, unpossessed, uncontained *Infinite AWARENESS-I! Who* says we are bound to the male outlook or the female outlook because "we were born that way"? Who says we see everything as either good or bad because that is the nature of the beast? Who says Identity is either enlightened or unenlightened, expanded or unexpanded, developed or undeveloped, awake or sleeping? Who is twisting our arm and making us *continue* those beliefs? Not God, not Reality, not Wholeness, not Allness, not Awareness!

We stop identifying as half the pendulum's swing, as half of All. Awareness (Identity) is COMPLETE. We stop thinking of ourselves as male, female, good, bad, enlightened, unenlightened, awake or sleeping. We do not have to think in that sense at all. We simply look—watch—behold—be; and find our *former* view of Life with *its* apparent contradistinction (death) appearing in new perspective.

CHAPTER XX

Life In The Light Of Contradistinction

The following essay comes in partial answer to requests that I write about the appearance of death. The study of this selection should be preceded by a thoughtful review of the selection on contradistinction and death, pages 175-179 in AWARENESS AND TRANQUILLITY, and a short period of introspective Self-writing (about LIFE, not death).

"Life" and "awareness" are the same living. The terms are identical. Living is the action of God. It may be said that Life is the knowing of Mind. That is, the awareness presently reading these words is the unconfined intelligence of *infinite* Mind. And this is so. Reader, what greater birthright could we have?

Because Mind is one, so is its action, Life—as shown by the fact that our Identity as awareness is primary, and all form appears within (as) this single consciousness of being.

The knowledge that this awareness is eternal reveals certain aspects of the "last enemy," what it is and why it appears as it does. Life's contradistinction, called death, is neither binding nor bad. Infinite Wisdom's knowledge of all that Life *IS* equally includes the intellectual knowledge of that which Life IS NOT—in the same way that the tangible view of yon pine did once and may again bring to mind a host of "is nots": i.e., that pine is not an oak, is not a hickory; a means (perhaps *the* means) by which the *IS* of that image (tree) is known *without doubt or equivocation.*

The contradistinctions that make the tree apparent are many, but as we approach Awareness—this single Center of Being—the contradistinctions lessen. It is upon the perception of the ONENESS that Awareness IS that we find (and understand) the *single* contradistinction by means of which this Awareness is KNOWN to be unending—the single contradistinction that awareness *is not:* non-awareness, non-life, death. (Just as Light has *one* final contradistinction: "is *not* Light" which we call darkness.)

For this reason, the final "is not" has been called the last enemy, but it is not an enemy at all. It is nothing to fear nor cringe before. It is naught more than the tangible appearing of a powerless contradistinction by which ETERNITY is perceived *beyond intellectuality and intellectuality's limits.* It can do no more to Life than the "is not oak" can do to our pine. (If you enjoy arithmetic, ask yourself how ETERNAL *Infinity* can appear *tangibly* EXCEPT as "periods" of "time"? Herein lies the answer to many a human mystery.)

STORMS

I was in Mississippi among my great oaks and pines when the hurricane called Camille blew over me. "Only with thine eyes shalt thou behold and see the reward of the (illusion) . . . there shall no evil befall thee, neither shall any plague come nigh thy dwelling. For he shall give his angels charge over thee, to keep thee in all thy ways. They shall bear thee up in their hands lest thou dash thy foot against a stone."

If there should be a storm in our affairs, whatever its appearance, it is there for a reason—and a good reason; not a bad one. The moments of tumult are Tranquillity's contradistinction wherein all that Tranquillity *is* becomes known beyond theory, *beyond* speculation and beyond every aspect of intellectuality.

Awareness is Mind's knowing of Mind. *Infinite* Mind's Self-awareness is unlimited, unbound. WE are this Wisdom, reader! Is it not awareness (life) that watches the thundering surf? Is it not life that feels the warm hand of friendship? Is it not life that looks into the night sky, watches the gathering clouds of a Summer shower and listens to the newly freed cicada as he sings to his love? And is it not that same consciousness that reads these words? It is. It is. The UNBOUND self-knowing of MIND!

As infinite wisdom, we come to find ourselves knowing what we should, as we should. Wisdom knows this paper is not a hickory leaf, is not a "porky-pine" and is not a blue-eyed little girl. The "is nots" are never what the paper *is*—yet they serve to make the distinction clear if and when such a distinction seems necessary in our affairs. While they sometimes appear as direful, foreboding events, they have no power nor authority for aught but *good*. The prior events of our life have never been fatal. The awareness that reads these words will never stop being the activity of being Deity's Self-consciousness, called Life. This Life that awareness is is an eternal Watch from Glory to ever more expansive Glory!

Once, in war, I watched the slaughter of a valley of people. Death appeared on every hand. Women cried. Children screamed. Men shouted in fear and agony. I was a soldier there, frightened like all the rest. In the midst of the carnage, seemingly out of the press of fear on the one hand and an abiding faith on the other that surely a good God's design could never include such a scene as this, as *only* this, I was introduced to a view on the "other side" of death's appearance—a fuller view than the ordinary. Then, I could not explain that event nor understand all it revealed, but since that time the affairs of "my" life have been an unending explanation as though I were in class, given instruction by angels, by the sun and stars, by a still small voice, by a Holy Muse and a gentle wind from out the camp site of a New Day on the river of life.

Those of you who are afraid, listen:

"Only with thine eyes shalt thou behold and see . . ."

"Thou shalt NOT be afraid . . . it shall NOT come nigh thee . . ."

"His angels shall bear thee up in their hands."

These are things I know. The light of a distant galaxy only rushes into and past the *boundaries* of a *measured* earth. It does not end. Neither does the Light of Life end because of *Eternity's* contradistinction called "time."

      LOVE and LIGHT are eternal.

Dear Mary and John,

Two days out in the woods! Hunting arrowheads, walking Winter fields, feeling the January chill on my face.

A few years ago, Ruby and I were beating our way along the Buttahatchie looking for old Indian sites and arrowheads when we happened onto Mr. Johnson, a Mississippi farmer. When he found out what we were doing and that we were "none of them Yankee furiners," he took us over to a cornfield where some of the prettiest corn you've ever seen was standing twelve feet high. "Now, go on back thar in the middle of the field," he said, "'til ya come to a rise. If'n ya look good, I 'speck ya'll 'll find some 'ars (arrows)."

We did! His cornfield was smack on top of a burial mound and there were arrows all over the place!

Well, that's where I've been yesterday and today. And, John, finding an arrow that is still unbroken is about like landing a five-pound bass. My find today was fifteen beauties and I came back bearded, dirty, cold and miserable—eyes watering, nose running, muddy feet very tired. Great, just great!

I looked for arrows where aboriginal man lived. The world says they are dead and gone, but they are no such thing. Life lives for a time looking outward at things; then inward at That which is being things. Life is both views and they are much more simultaneous than is imagined, but the "thing-view" sees finiteness—and finiteness involves time and its succession. *The view within does not preclude the vision of finite things; rather, it includes it to infinity.*

The personal, finite view of "death" is not the final say in the matter. We live our world until we live it perfectly. Our first and last step in this regard is the shedding of the personal sense of self—the ego—the selfhood apart from the One. But even this is but barely a matter of our own doing. For me it has seemed much more an action of letting, of being, of watching, of nonaction in the human sense.

Well, once before, looking for arrows—that time in the Spring—tired and thirsty I bent myself down to drink from a pond, and there reflected in the water He was—in my own image He was...

Unlimited, unbound Love to you both!

CHAPTER XXI

Deathless Life

THE FINAL LESSON LEARNED

We find that every contradistinction relative to the nature of death, well being, supply, etc., falls away when the lesson of that contrary is learned. When we see that agony is the contrary pointing out Joy, the agony is seen for what it is, vanishes, and the "higher" order of being presents itself. When "lack" is found to be the contrary proving our eternal Sufficiency, the appearance of lack vanishes into its native nothingness. Exactly so, when we clearly perceive the answers to the problems written on the blackboard, the problems that present themselves for the proving are erased, the examination is over and we leave the shadows of the classroom for the unlimited sunshine where no more problems exist.

Now we are finally facing up to the "final enemy" to be "destroyed." We see "death" as the obvious, natural, harmless (and mathematically precise) final contrary whereby

Awareness KNOWS Awareness to be eternal. Futhermore, it is our inexorable *proof* of eternal Awareness, inasmuch as *every* human science is delineated finitely by means of contradistinction.

If every observable, feelable, hearable object that we have ever been aware of has made its presence known *tangibly* by means of contraries (and all human science will verify the fact that this is so), we know that Awareness's final examination of its eternality is "known" in exactly the same way. That "final" contrary, called "death," is no more able to end LIFE than "is not pine" can strip the limbs from oak.

Awareness concedes these points as a Child, surrenders all ego-argument to the contrary and the blackboard with death's enigma is erased. Sorrow and sighing flee and death seems no more.

THE HORSEMAN AND THE BOY

He gave the screw another turn. The wood cracked slightly and puffed over the top of the screw. Everyone watched with intent interest except the little boy in the rear of the room. He was looking out the window, down the road, past the ramshackledy house and to the hill beyond.

The man gave another turn and the splitting wood could be heard across the room. The boy looked away from the window to the faces of those who watched the man standing over the coffin. He looked into every face and noted that not a one was aware of him; then he looked out the window again to the hill beyond the ramshackledy house.

"By gosh, that oughta hold it!" said one of the on-lookers.

"It ought to, but I'm gonna put in another," said the man who was putting the huge screws into the coffin. He took another of the mammoth pieces of threaded metal from the box at his feet and prepared to start it into the side of the coffin with a heavy hammer.

With the sound of the first blow the little boy turned from the window again. He noticed the attention of the onlookers was beginning to waver. At any moment one of them would see him there in the rear of the room standing half in the sunlight from the window and half in the shadows of the old country store. "I wish he would come," he whispered to himself, and made another survey of the hill beyond the ramshackledy house. Then his face lifted in an eager smile. Coming over the hill rode a tall man sitting stiff and straight in the saddle, leaning forward in that half arrogant, half swashbuckling way that nobody on earth but his father had. "It's him! It ain't nobody but him!" the lad all but shouted aloud, and he would have if it hadn't been for the people around the child's coffin at the front of the store.

"Poor kid," the man with the tool said. "You'd have thought he just didn't care the way he jumped offa that ledge at the quarry.

"I don't think he did care. He didn't care for nothin' since his pa was killed at Gettysburg. He didn't have no ma and his brothers are off fightin'. The way he loved that pa of his, I just don't think he cared. He just laughed when we told him he couldn't make it over that ledge below. He said his pa could do it and if'n his pa could he reckoned he could, too."

The boy in back of the room had moved to the window and leaned out as if to hurry the distant horseman. His eyes, alight, were filled with tears and they cleaned a path through the dirty, sweaty cheeks, rolled under his chin and made a dark spot on the scrubbed wood sill of the window. "It's him," he whispered to himself through excitement-clenched teeth. "It's him. I'd know that ride any day of the week and twicet on Sunday!"

The work on the coffin had stopped and those closest gathered around it and lifted it gently from the workbench. A solemn procession moved slowly toward the door.

The boy by the window turned, frightened now that he would be seen. Quickly wiping his sleeve across his nose and cheek in an effort to wipe away the tearful evidence, he prepared to speak. Then he noticed that still no one was looking at him; except there was old James, he was looking at him; but sorta looking right through him, too, like he didn't see him at all. None of them looked like they saw him. "They're so filled with sadness, I reckon," the boy thought. "They just don't see me atall — like they never did hardly see me — but nobody pays no attention to a boy."

The procession with the coffin left. Out by the tree, just before their voices would have been out of range, someone said, "He just jumped off'n that high ledge yellin', 'Come and git me, Pa! I'd druther be with you!' I think he was plumb crazy with loneliness."

The tall rider and white horse were approaching the old store. The boy turned from the sight of the solemn procession carrying the coffin and ran to greet the swashbuckling Confederate officer riding so high in the saddle.

"Eddie!" yelled the rider.

"Pa!" answered the little boy.

Barely reining his big white horse, the soldier leaned in the saddle and grabbed the boy on the run. Tears streaming from the eyes of both, their embrace was a father and son reunion. The boy held on, squeezing with the unabashed love of a little boy so long separated from his father. The lathered horse snorted and pawed the ground.

"Oh, Pa. Pa!" he said. "I love you, Pa!"

"I love you, too, Eddie. I've missed you so much."

"I've missed you, too. But now we're together, Pa!"

"Yes, we're together, and this time we'll stay together."

He prodded the horse into a slow walk and turned up the street toward the church. The brief funeral had ended and the procession carrying the small coffin left the church and headed toward the cemetery at the side.

"Pa," said the small boy on horseback, "they never did pay no attention to me at all 'til I jumped off'n that ledge."

"I know, son," said his father, "but we're together now."

By any language I can muster, I make the point that death is naught but the tangibly appearing contradistinction by means of which the intellect of us perceives the ETERNALITY OF LIFE — and knows it knows beyond all doubt. What does infinite Wisdom *not* know?

The *Awareness* that reads these words will never experience "death" any more than LIGHT will ever experience darkness, the contradistinction by means of which Light is tangibly comprehended. We note that the power lies with light, the least spark of which cannot be subdued by all the darkness in the universe.

Death is what intelligent Life knows it is not and could never be. As the old Taoists say, "With the Light of Life, there is no end!" And there isn't.

For those who are becoming alive to the real Identity, the examination is soon to be over. The *tangible* evidence of Life's omnipresence shall reveal that no soldier, no way-farer, no stranger, no friend, child or loved one has ever died. And, gentle reader, you will feel, hear and see that this is so! Omnipresence is not excluded from the "many rooms" of its own being.

Before proceeding with this volume, make your-self *reread* the preceeding three chapters on "contra-distinction." You will be surprised to find them say-ing quite something else with the second reading — more, much more, than the feeble words.

CHAPTER XXII

A Course Of Action In The Midst Of Turmoil

Reader, the following is an essay of urgency pertaining to the events of the day and "what to do" concerning them. I have been urged from within to get it written, but it has not been easy to find the words. Even after many revisions I am aware it barely touches the hem of the Light I have been given to see and tell about.

The *seed* is here, however—the gist. The discerning Heart, the Single Eye, will find it and ascertain its significance relative to the great crunch soon to be brought to bear against the established ideas of the world—all of them—religious, educational, political, monetary, social, et al—awesome events perhaps, but nothing to be frightened of, nothing that can harm Identity.

As simple, unjudging Awareness, we can watch it all with wonder and excitement like children standing on a high peak surveying the pounding surf below. The storm passes and the earth is refreshed. The Real remains untouched.

The honest action of our daily experience appears to be a quiet middle ground, a delicate balance. Consider, for instance, the cautious balance between *not yielding* and *not contending*—or *not contending* and *not yielding*.

In the human scheme of things, the refusal to yield to something we have come to perceive as a false authority is accompanied by the world's moral demand to do battle with that authority and set it straight—always for the idealistic benefit of others, of course. Such action is the product of human "education" and has become the intuitive reflex of a society geared to "progress." But there is another course of action open to us wherein we quietly refuse to yield to any authority but the Divine, yet remain careful (for our own peace and the benefit of the world) not to overstep that refusal thence to begin *contending* with the binding, confining false authority.

Of course, the world holds this course in grand contempt. Even the world's metaphysicians, by and large, attempt to rectify appearances, but our *tangible* freedom in daily experience will never be found outside this delicate balance between not yielding and not contending.

No, we do not cow before the supposed power of images, signs and symbols, that have no power; we do not act as floor mats nor yield ourselves servants to obey the appearances of the world and its sundry enslaving ideas. But neither do we take those actions that constitute a battle with the world's pseudo-authority. When this delicate point is perceived and lived (and *lived!*) our vision of war, rebellion and personal inharmony is ended.

BY WAY OF EXPLANATION

A growing portion of my correspondence concerns itself as follows: (1) "Our children (or grandchildren) are anti-establishment, anti-adult, anti-social and contemptuous of nearly everything conventional. All they are *for* are mind-changing drugs. *What am I to do?"* (2) "My organization (school, business, church, body) is woefully caught up in the dictatorial emptiness of old conditioned thinking and would attempt to enslave me thereby. What am I to do, pull up stakes or battle for an improvement in my organization?"

As appearances go, our response to the second question has given rise to the appearances that motivate the first. The answer to the one is the answer to the other—but that answer does not exist out there with rebellious society and its destructive actions, nor with the recalcitrant, dictatorial organizations so many would like to see reorganized to fit a new pattern. It has altogether to do with this action the *reader* is right here—no one else and nowhere else. One does not *have* to "pull up stakes" *or* "battle for an improvement." There is yet another course of action, a barely seen *center ground* upon which one may stand and find himself having cleared up both situations for himself at once. As this action-WE-are stops its battle with its "out there," we see the *meaning* behind the world's turmoil and see it without fear or loss of equanimity.

For me it has been helpful to learn the hard lesson that challenging the pseudo-powers of the world does not mean a battle. To challenge the authority of a power that is *not* God is to stand firm on the single ground of *God's* omnipotence, therein discovering the powerlessness of the pseudo-authority—and finding it in the first hand language of my own experience.

To battle with the pseudo-authority in either action or argument is to give it (in my own experience) the very power it does not possess outside my belief that it is a power to overcome, change, heal or, as I am sometimes tempted, paste in the mouth with a tomato—as if there *could* be a power besides God! Even then, the battle is with a *belief—a personal* determination that a power besides God exists capable of binding us and doing us in.

The faltering heart, the swollen joints, the fractious groups and warring nations are the evidence of that fictitious belief. To see the end of the mischief "there," *we* end the contention with our *own* images "here." Reader, you see this?

It is not the people in our world who must do this. Rather, this consciousness that "includes" those people does it *first, then* we see our mirrored Self-images doing likewise. We be the lifted up, pristine Awareness smiling at itself *here* and find ourselves living the Christ of our Self-perceived, Self-inclusive universe smiling back from the mirror.

The images of perception, whether they be institutions, people or feelings, are not the masters of the consciousness (Life) reading these words. Rather, institutions, people, feelings have their apparent existence because ISNESS (God) is aware *as* this awareness we are. Dominion resides where *this* one exists. To be dictated to by a false authority is to yield oneself servant thereof and sleep enslaved. To let our own images lead us around by the nose just because "they say" thus and so is as senseless as the television set that trembles in fear that one of its images will smash the picture tube. We question the basic authority of the slavemaster by understanding the *reasons* for its appearance in our affairs.

Yes, lest we be fooled and find ourselves adding to the picture's agony rather than *seeing* the naught of it, we awaken to the narrow pathway between the challenge of external authority that would bind us, and doing battle with it. The present rebellion of certain groups within "society" will stop its senseless destructiveness and come out from its subverting, perverting nastiness only as this awareness-being-I ends its *own* contention with its included images. Within the cause-effect arena of mental manipulation, the appearance of a society being ripped apart by guilt-ridden groups demanding freedom is the inevitable consequence of our own vain effort at mental manipulation—attempts to elevate a mistaken sense of Self up to a Perfection that is already All. He who would try to improve the world, spoils it, as Laotse said.

The time is ripe to stand fast as the witness of the ALLNESS we know to be the Fact of existence. *We* pull in the insensate reins of contention *here*-as-I-within before we can understand why our images appear to be going off half cocked in all directions. We live and act the Christ-Comforter we are to our own perception of existence first.

We do not save our world by doing battle with it, tearing it down, burning it up, creating doubt or suspicion, undermining it, healing it, manipulating it or trying to resign from it via a letter of resignation or drugs. We "save" it by seeing it as it is, seeing ourselves as we are, and acknowledging ISNESS to be the basis for all that is, has been, or could be.

WHERE THE AUTHORITY IS

God, the reality being this single and only AWARENESS I AM, is the authority that blooms the bud, scatters the seed and flashes its Cosmic Light around the universe. This authority has never been vested in a human organization, be it a body with organs, a scientific institution, a financial institution, a marriage institution or a smother church. Furthermore, none of us has ever been unfaithful to this Divine Authority being Identity, nor "lapsed from the faith." How, in God's allness, can Identity lapse from Itself?

Undoubtedly, organizations (even as the body) perform legitimate, worthwhile services, but those services are abrogated to whatever extent we give the organization power to enslave its members *or to whatever extent we claim a position of superiority* or inferiority for *our own appearances of organization* or views of Reality.

Isness, not people, is the genuine authority for individual action. The consciousness that reads these words stands as its own self-evident proof of being, Deity's awareness of existence. Its relationship to Being is not governed by the man-made laws of *any* intermediary, no matter how correctly (Divinely) authorized it is or professes to be. The communion between Reality and this consciousness-we-are is not now, and has never been, routed through any external church, philosophy, system, leader, ritual, institution or book—to include the Bible. Intercourse with Reality is *direct,* as direct as Allness is ever its own sameness. Enlightenment, the "mysterious agreement," is between IS and AM, the single ONE, Self-evident to and as *this* Awareness-I-am. My proof of this fact is the Light I live as, and see enlightening my Experience.

When this is understood, we find our Light appearing on the scene via books, institutions, friends and strangers at every turn of the road—and we know when *that* appearing *is* our own Within disclosing Itself to us in the language of the moment.

The "authority of the organization," whatever its appearing, resides in That being THIS consciousness. That which presents itself as intermediary—pope, church, institution, society, bible or canon of ancient law—exists powerlessly in "us" (Me) as images of *this* awareness-I-am.

"SO WHAT DO I DO ABOUT MEMBERSHIP IN MY COLLEGE (OR CHURCH OR BUSINESS OR WORLD)?"

The Golden Thread of the Absolute exists. We know because we have found it. We feel, know and see the Fact of Singleness—evidence of God's ALLNESS. We who discern the Thread are come as the savior of our own appearing, the Christ to the Experience we are.

As I see it now, it makes no difference whether we are inside an organization or outside it, provided we do not feel a sense of restriction. Even then, cutting ourselves away does not mean we will find the restriction gone. It is the sense of being an identity *capable of being restricted* that appears to me as a "me" bound by an ailing body, oppressive organization or a flat pocketbook. The axe at the root has to do with *this* one's position, not the "Church's." Identity is a matter of SELF determination and in the end, no organization, not even the body, can prevent the discovery.

Therefore, I do not presume to tell anyone whether he should join an organization or leave one. We each follow what seems the Heart-directed course of action. For myself, I once thought the wisteria vine was the most beautiful of all the flowers in the garden. As a gardener, I worked with my wisteria to the exclusion of all else and awakened one day entangled, no longer free to follow the sunlight outside the shadows. For *me* (though not necessarily for thee) it seemed wise to come out and be separate from that clinging vine because I could neither speak nor write of my own self-unfoldments without violating rules to which I had willingly agreed. So I cut myself away from the organizational rules and

found the more distant purview of the wisteria lovelier
than ever! More: I found the beauty of the orchid!
I found the larkspur, the rose, the dandelion, the sassafras
root and the wild woodland outside the regulated bound-
ary of the garden!

Every flower in the garden is ME and I take my nectar
from any book or blossom I see I be at the moment.
Only those organizations that permit such freedom can
survive.

In all fairness I must point out again that my entanglement with the wisteria of old theology was not the wisteria's fault. A vine is a vine—neither good, bad, right
nor wrong—but who can make wisteria into heather or a
dandelion into a rose? If there isn't enough shade beneath
the pine, we sit under an oak, but we don't cut down the
pine nor strip it of its limbs. Its shade may be quite
enough for the tufted titmouse, the bushy-tailed squirrel
or the mercenary who thinks *that* tree is the only tree
capable of dropping an "apple" in his lap.

Which is easier: to play the role of a great crusading
contender doing impossible (and miserable) battle with
society and its organizations, or to stop playing that role
and rest in the happy Already? For myself, I prefer to
let pine trees be pine trees and wisteria vines be wisteria
vines. If, in blaming the vine for my own entanglement,
I should succeed in pulling it up by the roots, what will
I have to show for it except a hernia, a sore back and the
sight of a wrecked society ripped apart by excessive
zealousness?

God's Phoenix of ALREADY does not *have* to rise
from the ruins of a shattered society. It will appear to,
of course, but those who know the forthright way of the
middle ground—of the *already* Infinite—will not be trou-

bled as the dream's last soliloquy is sounded, as the curtain falls with a crash and the mortal arc lights give way to the Light of the Eternal, sunshine of the Real.

CHAPTER XXIII

Ecclesiasticism And Identity

The old nature of us has been built up over a long period. It has developed thousands of supports, props, crutches. A real or imaginary attack against any of these supports produces an ego shock accompanied by a protective reflex as instinctive and natural as batting an eye or brushing away a stinging wasp. The ego lashes out at the merest hint of a threat to any of its crutches and will whale the daylights out of an imaginary affront that doesn't even exist yet. Such is the nature of the world's vaunted "self-esteem."

This ego is natural for all of us, however, and exists in its season as the Selfhood's contradistinction whereby the Real is *known* in more than theory. Does not the tangible appearing of *infinite* Wisdom require a knowledge of the "is nots"? "Life is *not* finite! Life is *not* bound to a body! Life is *not* limited."

The crutches are, every one, ultimately removed. They must be and will be *seen* to support an *unreal* identity. It is for this reason that every action of *mankind* appears self-destructive.

He perishes like the grass, having only endured a season.

"Awakening" and all that word implies, is our arrival at a knowledge of the real Identity as opposed to the contradistinctive-ego, that miserable bag of bones, tissue, pumps and water, of few days and full of trouble. We are driven to this awakening by the collapse of ego *props*—if not in this time, in another—until such time as the old man hasn't a leg to stand on, the deterioration of his body or affairs opening his eyes to a grander dimension, considerably wider and more beautiful than the narrow world his instinctive ego-protective reflexes allow him to see.

Statements of metaphysical Truth come to call attention to the Primal Selfhood which exists in mathematical terms as diametrically "equal and opposite" (contradistinctive) to our world-educated view of identity. Statements relating to the Primal Identity come as crutch *removers* to the misidentification even while that one is busily acquainting himself with the cause and effect aspect of metaphysics attempting to turn it into a new crutch, a new hope and a way to solve human problems. The ego clutches the asp of its own destruction. It drinks the hemlock of its own demise. *Misstatements* of the Absolute may be twisted into popular theologies and philosophies ("The power of your mind," "How to visualize and create wealth," "How to *use* the truth to do to this or that"), but the Absolute cannot possibly be *intellectually* popular. Yet neither can the Heart-real of mankind be prevented from eventually hearing and recognizing the real Self.

This is why the *clearly delineated* Truth of Being is not relished by our human view of mankind and why he has developed such a sense of blindness toward all he instinctively knows will do him in. This is why his organizations build mystical shells around the Primal Identity whose Light eliminates the shadow of its inversion—the ego and its organizations to which it yields itself a servant to obey. But even this is the only way it can appear "in the world." Contradistinctions of the Infinite present themselves finitely, hence tangibly, and since they are finite, they are bound to sequence and its time.

The questions arise: What is the *present* "role" of the Absolute? Why should we study something that is so obviously ego-destructive? Why rush things if the ego sense will vanish anyway, since its supports are ultimately found to be false supports of an introverted sense of Self?

"Time" will disclose just how important the single answer to these questions is. The answer is simple even though the words and illustrations to make it intellectually acceptable are virtually impossible at this time. This much has been clearly shown: when the "reasons" for the tangible contradistinction becomes apparent, the "need" for the contradistinction has ended—the suffering goes out of it and our fear is ended forever. An unshakeable Tranquillity discloses itself, which, among other things, is the basis for "healing" in the world. More, it is the Light of Identity humanity is searching for. We can say, as Jesus did, "I am the Light of the world" and "I have overcome the world."

And you, reader? You have the same mission, the same grand task, the same holy heritage to awaken and find yourself the *seeing* of God, the Awareness of Reality. Then, this seen, it is to *act* as the seeing directs.

FREEDOM

During the final days already in progress the dissolution of all that stands between ourselves and a full knowledge of the Truth will come. The Light is already here. New ideas are coming into *common* focus and old landmarks are being taken away. Cherished notions, oft the pillars of society, are crumbling with the shifting sand they stand on.

Everything that appears to hold mankind in bondage will finally give way. Freedom will out. The New Light is irresistible because it is already the only real fact.

As usual, many of the institutions whose first purpose was to tend the New Vine of Life as it broke forth into the Garden are now busily trying to confine that infinite vine to their narrow plots, pruning every new shoot and burning every seed the vine produces. Even as in days of yore, intellectual pomposity would attempt to regulate and administer the Light rather than *be* the Light—and like dogs in the manger, neither eat the oats nor let the oxen eat. Often the minister, the practitioner or the simple honest student who would labor for love of the Vine, rather than for the plot within which it appears to grow, finds himself alienated by the body of laws developed through the years to regulate the conduct of the gardeners —the Vine itself having long been lost sight of by the caretakers of the plot and their walls of human regulations. However, as appearances go, those walls are coming down too, being cracked asunder by the same infinite and eternal Vine which cannot be pruned. Neither can it be held to an old position.

———

There is the story of a palatial institution whose many members were constantly giving their poor gardener the devil. Half the members objected when the gardener turned the water sprinkler on and the other half objected when he turned it off. Furthermore, those who wanted him to turn it on objected to the *way* he did it and those who did *not* want him to turn it on objected to the way he did *not* do it.

All the while, the honest and faithful gardener (minister, reader, practitioner, student or janitor) went on enjoying the flowers until he or she was harassed into quitting, thence to run to that infinite Garden out along the edge of the woodland where no walls have ever been built and none will ever be seen tumbling down.

The Garden is the very consciousness that reads these words. Who or what can hold it in bondage?

CHAPTER XXIV

About Liars

Youth is calling for honesty. Honest *actions*. Honesty is coming into focus, called to our attention by the apparent dishonesties at every point on the human scene.

I knew a woman who was driving herself insane over her husband's and daughter's proclivity for lying. "They lie about everything," she told me in great anguish. "Jack is an inveterate, congenital liar who can't tell the truth even when he tries and Jane is getting just like him. He lies to me about his business and where he goes and what he does. He lies about everything. Now, Jane is following in his footsteps and it is just killing me. I'm going out of my mind. His lying is destroying this marriage and me with it."

A word is a word is a word. A word cannot be Truth *itself*, but, at the very most, only a statement *about* Truth. Truth is being words, but words are not, and cannot be, all there is to *truth*. Therefore, all words are relative and cannot be the Absolute *itself*. Despite the world court's demand for us to be truthful, *words* cannot be "the truth, the whole truth and nothing but the truth" no matter what they say nor who says them. Never.

185

Generally speaking, we know this is so. For instance, we know when someone is talking about death that the words are about an illusion and "above and beyond" those words there is an eternal Life. We know when we are called on for "help" that the declarations of woe, want, pain or anguish have little to do with the REAL. People say, "I *seem* to be unhappy but I know it really isn't how it seems. Will you help me see the real?" or words to that effect.

Behind the appearance of the tangible "thing" stands the ineffable, nameless, wordless, intangible *Isness being* the "thing." Behind every tangible word, written or spoken, stands the same Isness—an Isness considerably more than a personal determination of "honest" or "dishonest."

So, the lady began to listen for the *truth* which lay behind her family's words. She knew *that* Truth was changeless, perfect, non-destructive and incapable of destroying "Home." *Then* she saw the wonders that came from eliminating the labels she had hung on her own sense of husband and daughter. She saw the glory of forgiveness. "If there is Truth behind the sound of the words," she told me, "there is Truth behind the appearance of a husband, no matter *how* he acts or what he says. Now it is up to me to choose which husband is real: the symbol or that for which the symbol stands."

And, with remarkable strength, she did this, even while the appearance of a human husband went on lying through its teeth. *Then* the "healing" presented itself. Most of us want the proof of the Real before we are willing to acknowledge the *totality* of the Real—and, of course, it doesn't work that way.

On the human scene, the anguish of "lying" stems from the power we give what we call lies to hurt us or damage our own sense of self. If the word coming from the image "out there" doesn't correspond with our idea of what that image should say (or write) then we want to blame the image for own own *refusal* to see it perfectly. *On* Not our *inability* to see it perfectly—our refusal to!

The liar is never out there. The liar is the one who says an out there is botched and capable of hurting this perfect Here and Now.

While this is a true story, suppose I make an analogy to point out just how strong and courageous this woman's actions were—how difficult—how contrary to the world's way of doing—and how these actions appear absolutely insane to the world, and why one is so reluctant to *act* on them. Perhaps this illustration will make clear some of the paradox of metaphysics.

THE ILLUSTRATION OF THE BANK ROBBER

Instead of the hurt wife, we have a bank. Instead of the lying husband and daughter, we have a bank robber and his accomplice. The monumental *human* task of those of us who are called on to hear, tell of, or *act* on the Real, is to convince the bank (of which we are president) that "God is ALL," therefore, the bank is pure, perfect, invulnerable and *incapable* of being robbed— and to be convinced of this (or convince them) *even in the face of a robber and an accomplice who are tangibly robbing the bank with near impunity,* reducing its assets day after day after day while bank examiners are screaming from every corner that a tangible robber is indeed stealing the place blind. "Here are his photographs even while he's doing it!" shouts the lady president.

Where is the bank that is willing to believe its invincibility in the face of such evidence as this? (And where is the writer capable of the words which may induce them to?)

Oh, but this is only the beginning of what we, the bank, are being asked to do! We are being called on to believe an even more ludicrous set of circumstances and then to *act* on that absurd evidence in an even *more* absurd and unbelievable way—an action for which we have strength enough but to the intellect it appears simply too insane to consider.

Our analogy continues. After the bank has tried every human and spiritual means to stop the robber, it receives a printed message *from the robber himself.* In the very face of the evidence of his thievery he has the gall to write: "While you think that you are the *victim* and that I am *guilty,* I am telling you that you *are incapable* of really being robbed, and what you see as robbery is the karmic consequence or 'equal and opposite reaction' *of not acting as though you believe your own invulnerability.*"

Imagine! What an affront to the intellect this guy is! And now his message goes on to add: "Mrs. Banker, if you want to *see* me stop robbing you, leave me alone! Just *watch* me coming and going, hauling out sack after sack of your money; and instead of seeing me as a robber, see me as a pure and guiltless *symbol of your own attempt to be dishonest,* calling itself to your attention!" (Where is the shrewd, planning, calculating, protecting intellect that can buy *that?*) "First, look on me as just a robber being a robber, *incapable* of stealing your *real* wealth— and then *act on your beliefs.* When I see you *believe* you are really invulnerable—that is, when I see you acting as though God *were* all and *all*—you will see me (and your wealth) in an entirely new light." Then, like rubbing our nose in it, he signs the note, "Your *friend,* the robber."

There is a postscript. Listen with the Heart.

"I know you want to see me stop robbing the bank *before* you think you can believe that God is Good, but

I ask you: how would you know this fact *unlimitedly,* and *know* that you *know* it unlimitedly, until you *act* on it *as though it were true in the face of overwhelming evidence to the contrary???*

"In other words, your 'healing' depends on *actually* seeing this point of Truth as more important *and more valuable* than the price you place on all you think you are losing *or can* lose! In short, Mrs. Banker, this 'awful mess you are in' is not such a mess after all—but it will appear *until* you are willing to *live* your professions. Nothing less than that will be acceptable. You must make the supreme sacrifice, willing to surrender everything—and there is no way for you to *know* whether this is true or not until you have done it."

Show me the bank that can come to understand and *act* on this grand paradox and I will show you a bank that comprehends why Jesus was brought to exclaim, "Only one in a thousand, two in ten thousand . . ." and why that Carpenter of Love was forsaken by his every disciple, every one of them, when the chips were down and they were called on to put their professions into practice.

Reader, can you see what courage the woman had? She *acted* upon her conviction that God is All and the liar was naught but a liar, incapable of destroying her. Is it any wonder that her faithfulness was rewarded as a new view of her husband—first, ". . . as the grandest teacher of my life!" and then as a perfectly "normal" husband about the business of being a good husband?

That lady is a teacher herself today, bringing many to see the same point—and, of course, getting *called* an awful liar herself, in what comes as the intellectually painful process of her Self-images being seen to know what she knows.

To paraphrase a little: Let him who has Heart to hear this, hear this with the Heart he is.

ABOUT NAMES AND LABELS

What *name* is given this philosophy? What are these ideas called? Is this Christian Science? Is it Unity or Religious Science? Is it Taoism, Buddhism, Existentialism, Solipsism, Judaism? Is it The Infinite Way carried another step forward? Is this an Eastern philosophy or Western? Is it a combination of all of these or is it none?

"He that hath an ear, let him hear what the Spirit saith to the churches: To him that overcometh will I give to eat of the hidden manna, and will give him a white stone, and in the stone *a new name written, which no man knoweth saving he that receiveth it.*"

This study is related to no organization. It has grown out of no religious group. This is not a special theology more related to one church than another, or more to one metaphysics than another. The Truth is the Truth is the Truth—not strained *through* any organization. It follows no particular line of teachers. The Truth does not come *out* of any faith, organization, teacher, philosophy or holy book. The Truth *includes* all that has ever been construed to be any and every teacher, philosophy or holy book. The Truth we are concerned with is the truth of the Single Selfhood being the awareness of these words. There is one Truth only—the fact of Identity—the truth I am.

Jesus said: "Blessed are the solitary and elect, for you shall find the Kingdom . . ." That same enlightened mirror of my Self also said, "Many are standing at the door, but the *solitary* are the ones who will enter the bridal chamber. . . . He who lives *as* the *living one* shall see neither death nor fear . . ." This study is a matter of Self-discovery—an individual, solitary action. But one does not have to forsake business, friends, family nor society and its organizations to persue it. As Awareness,

I AM The Truth, I Am the Way, I Am The ONE I AM That I AM, without a second.

we are the Living *one* within whom the universe is included.

A year ago, a European Rabbi told me that I was teaching the Essene philosophy of Judaism in its purest form. The same week an "authority" announced that these ideas are the essence of Taoism. Time and again, those who know have said they are an absolutely correct statement of Christian Science. A recent letter states that A GUIDE TO AWARENESS AND TRANQUILLITY accords with the spirit of Buddhism. Many teachers of Unity, Religious Science and New Thought have come here to Mountain Brook to learn and say that these principles coincide with the most absolute aspects of their teaching. And I know that all of these statements are correct because Truth is *universal*—single, alone, only and all.

"But you haven't answered my question," said a young man to me a few days ago. "What do you *call* this teaching? What is its name?"

Names are labels. Labels are the names for specific things. Labels are for parts, bits and pieces, not for the single, whole, universal *all*. Labels have us looking out at something else with which we may or may not identify. Labels are for groups, organizations and philosophies which have followers. *But the truth we are has no limiting label on it*—unless we would limit ourselves. The Truth we are is the Identity we are. It is self-defeating to hang a label on it. The moment we do, we have *that* name standing in contradistinction to all other names; we have established an *ex*clusiveness rather than an inclusiveness; we see *this* Self-label as not *that* Self-label, which makes this self not *the* Self.

Regardless of the organizations, religious or otherwise, that we may belong to in order to avail ourselves of their intellectual instruction, camaraderie and kitchen facilities, our deepest and final study is *self* study, *self* discovery, *self* education and *self* acquaintance. It is defeating and dishonest to call ourselves by some limiting name which we are not.

It is well to remind ourselves that the awareness that reads these words or hears the sounds of labels is also the awareness that knows whatever is known of Judaism, Religious Science, The Infinite Way, Taoism, Catholicism, Christian Science or the American Automobile Association. Those concepts do not exist *outside* this *awareness* we are. They owe their apparent existence to the awareness that is conscious of them. They are subservient to *awareness,* the *selfhood* I (Identity) *am.* The labels are for the included images and ideas, for the parts, for the bits and pieces, the qualities and attributes, "the ten thousand things," for the flowers in the garden—for the birds—*but not for the one-I (we) am.* Who can give the Deific Identity a name? By what name does the Nameless go?

We break with the notion of being a part, to be the *whole,* the "Living *one."* Soon we shall all see that we are not members of this or that label, but that *every* label exists as some aspect of this Identity we are. And listen, listen: this knowledge does not mean that we *must* fight with or break from the sundry organizations that may appear meaningful to us at the moment. As a matter of fact, the knowledge that a label *cannot* bind the Identity we are may very well appear as that particular labeled aspect of ourselves becoming more meaningful than ever, in ways we never dreamed. And certainly, it means we would stop attempting to lower the boom on the rose just because it has thorns. We might even see that it was the rose's thorn that made us leap so high in the air we were able to see the *whole* garden of *many flowers.*

Semantic tricks to equate the comfortable old label of yore with the *unnamable identity*-we-are will ultimately be abandoned. We are all prone to slam the door in the face of certain labels as surely as we are to pucker at the taste of green persimmons or sigh at the sight of a little girl giving a flower to her daddy. We are here to find and live the *whole* Self we are and speak of *that.* This is why we search for a simplified, universal language that has neither crystalized nor been anchored to labels—and this study is proving itself capable of reaching *every* group we are being. Just today a letter arrives from one of the world's authorities on religion, Zen in particular, saying in essence that our messages are identical.

So, who can name this "way"? Who can label this single Selfhood except the Self *"you"* are? ". . . And I will give him . . . a white stone, and in the stone a *new* name written which no man knoweth saving he that receiveth it."

Asked the same question, Laotse answered: "I do not know Its name. If I *must* name It, I call it Tao and I hail it as supreme."

A FINAL WORD ABOUT MARRIAGE AND "ORGANIZATION"

Reader, you have seen many marital difficulties solved as you stopped pointing the finger of guilt to the other half "out there" and began to see *that* one as an aspect of the Self *you* are. Now, watch the happy wonders that will happen in your marriage *as you stop thinking of yourself as a member of the marriage institution!* To believe *that* is to yield yourself a servant who *can* be smothered by it. The Awareness that includes the organization has the dominion, not the organization. You are not a member of the marriage institution even though it may appear so. That institution is *your* member, an aspect of yourSelf. This is to see that the institution of human marriage does not have the authority to make us either happy or miserable, whether part of our experience or not!

Now, be cautious lest you let the intellect look on this as a threat to itself, under the guise of a threat to "home, family and marriage." The *dominion* of *Allness* is not a threat to *itself*, nor to anything that is real—and there is nothing real but Allness.   Holiness, Isness,

---

We do not belong to an organization no matter how many of them include our names on their roster of members. Rather, the organization, institution, fraternity or whatever, "belongs" to us, included within and as the Consciousness *we* are.

How can life belong to an idea it includes within itself? While the tangible point in time and space (called Bill or Mary) may "belong" to this or that organization for *intellectual* or social purposes (and there is nothing wrong with that!) that does not mean that *identity*-I has surrendered its heritage. *Our slowly arrived-at knowledge of this Fact is the start of the conscious recovery of our holy Birthright.* In Truth, it has never really been surrendered except in the binding, blinding *belief* that there is a medical fraternity, a scientific or religious organization, a marriage institution, a business and financial institution, a human society or a body organization to which we are subservient *members* and, therefore, supposed to bow down, salaam three times and do what "they" say or pay the consequences "they" dictate.

The dominion is *ours*. "And God gave man *dominion* . . ." "Know ye not that to whom ye yield yourselves servants to obey, his servants ye are . . .?" The New English Bible puts it: "You know well enough that *if you put yourself* at the disposal of a master, to obey him, you are *slaves* . . ."

Now, does this mean that we are to do battle with the appearances of "principalities and powers" "out there"? Not at all. It means that we see the Power *here as I*, not there as that. And then *act* in accord, *and then act in accord*.

"What if the institution will not permit me to act in accord?" Then we are forced to live (in order to *know*) that the institution has no authority to *prevent* the Self-*all*-is from *being* the Self-All-is. This is what is going on in the world of appearances right now. The only institutions that will survive the growing turmoil are those that yield up their pseudo-authority to let *ISNESS* be the Authority.

Now hear this: That yielding is not done out there with the appearance of the institution. It is done *here* as *this awareness we are!* Do you see this?

CHAPTER XXV

"It Is A Movement And A Rest"

There are times when we get gosh-awful tired of studying the "truth;" times when nothing sounds right and when the inspirational thoughts of old fail us. I have put aside many papers and slammed shut many books during those recurring times when the fire of enthusiasm seemed to go out. It happens to all of us, reader, and when it does the darkness seems exceedingly dark, our hopelessness very real.

But be of good cheer. It happens for a reason. Listen:

Try as we might, we are still prone to study with a deeply ingrained misconception of ourselves. Out of old habit we pursue the Truth as though we are empty, ignorant sponges soaking up knowledge. Study is an inputting time. For the input—much like the pendulum swinging in one direction—there must be an equal and opposite action when the pendulum returns. Inputting study demands an equal output, *practicing* what we profess, *being* what we have learned—and by being, freely *giving* what we have received.

So, when you seem to enter the desolate doldrums and are faced with the drearies, put the books aside; lay down the pen. Look out at the sunshine. Look up at the Light.

Get up. Get *out*. Head for a pathway and go for a stroll. Listen for the soft sounds of love and laughter. Listen for the excitement of children at play. Listen to the wind in the treetops. Listen to the Heart. For a time, let go the meticulous logic of metaphysics and stop following the thoughts that weigh so heavily and cut so deeply. Dream for a time; like a child, daydream with abandon.

If you do these things, I assure you it will not be long until the Heart sings again. Not immediately, perhaps, but by evening; by the next morning; soon, sooner than otherwise. *Just do not be distraught* if your books go blank and your enthusiasm wanes, as the sincere are all too prone to do. Be patient and be assured the out-putting time will do the trick.

In addition I could tell you to find someone to do something for—to give a small gift to someone—to get into a happy conversation about the Truth. I could tell you to find some moist earth to sink your hands into or to walk barefoot on, or to bend your back in the sunshine until you are hot and wet. These things have a way of lightening the Heart and getting the garden weeded at the same time.

Take heart. The Spirit will soar and sing again. You see, the sparrow flies for a time and rests for a time. So do the Seasons. So does the Heart.

"It is a movement and a rest," said Jesus.

CONCLUSION

Once upon a time an aspiring artist walked twelve miles every week to study with a master. After some months, the master taught the student to perceive subtle shades of color he had never noticed before. The long walk become new and more beautiful.

Once upon a time an old man who had lived in the forest all his life learned the difference between a white oak and a water oak. The forest became new.

The next year he learned the difference between a post oak and a blackjack. The woodland became new still again.

Once upon a time I read a book containing a thousand pages. On the nine-hundred-and-ninety-ninth page, the doors of my Heart were opened and I perceived a ray of Light unperceived before. The nine-hundred-and-ninety-nine pages already read became brand new, *unread* and *unseen* by the New Light just revealed. Suddenly it was another walk, another woodland, another book of many awaiting new Scenes.

Gentle reader, Light of Light, read the words of this volume again—all of them. It will be another book. The Love between the lines will reveal itself *as* you. The words are not important but the Love undergirding them will, line upon line, precept upon precept, here a little, there a little, disclose your freedom and independence, your pristine beauty and uprightness. You and your world will become new again—and again.

Watch and see!

Love to you from Lollygog, adrift on the still waters of my river.

Unbound love to you from Lollygog, adrift on the still waters of my river.